Alpha and Omega

Meditations on the Divine Mystery

Volume II

Hawfields Press
Mebane, North Carolina
2011

Printed in the United States of America on acid-free paper.

First Edition

Front cover photo used with permission of NASA, ESA, and A. Nota (STScI/ESA)

Back cover photo used with permission of NASA, ESA, R. O'Connell (University of Virginia), F. Paresce (National Institute for Astrophysics, Bologna, Italy), E. Young (Universities Space Research Association/Ames Research Center), the WFC3 Science Oversight Committee, and the Hubble Heritage Team (STScI/AURA)

Alpha and Omega

Meditations on the Divine Mystery

Volume II

Louis E. Bauer

This collection is dedicated

to the memory of

Phillip Gerdes

Who Beheld the Divine Mystery

and was

Faithful to the Confessions of the Lutheran Church

Preface

A number of years ago, the great German theologian, Paul Tillich, wrote a collection of essays entitled, *The Shaking of the Foundations*. Tillich urged his reader to see that our international psyche and civilization, along with the very earth itself, were crumbling at their foundations. The good, the beautiful, and the loving were being suffocated by the dust of this shaking of and collapse of civilization. He invites readers to consider the following, from the prophet, Isaiah:

> *The foundations of the earth do shake. Earth breaks to pieces,*
> *earth is split in pieces, earth shakes to pieces, earth reels like*
> *a drunken man, earth rocks like a hammock; under the weight*
> *of its transgression earth falls down to rise no more!*

Isaiah 24:18-20

Tillich writes, "It is hard to speak after the prophets have spoken as they have in these pronouncements. Every word is like the stroke of a hammer. There was a time when we could listen to such words without much feeling and without understanding. There were decades and even centuries when we did not take them seriously. Those days are gone. Today we must take them seriously. For they describe with visionary power what the majority of human beings in our period have experienced, and what, perhaps in a not too distant future, all mankind will experience abundantly. 'The foundations of the earth do shake.' The visions of the prophets have become an actual, physical possibility, and might become an historical reality. The phrase, 'Earth is split in pieces,' is not merely a poetic metaphor for us, but a hard reality. That is the religious meaning of the age into which we have entered."

* * *

In our own twenty-first century world, these harsh, apocalyptic words capture the reality of our foundations shaking to piles of dust, scattered to the four winds. But to envision this harshness clearly is also to open our blinded eyes to another light: the cross of Jesus the Christ. In the darkness of our psyches or the darkness of the cosmos, a light shines with the beauty of self-sacrificing love and grace. Only by standing tall in this light can we withstand the shaking and crumbling of our foundations. Only the grace of the Divine Mystery can shelter and protect us from the shards of history and keep us, and the creation, pure and holy.

Phillip Gerdes, my dear friend from Charlotte, North Carolina, grasped this Divine Mystery and lived boldly in the shadow of the cross of Christ. To the memory of this life, these meditations are dedicated with great affection.

My children, Jason and Megan, and my grandchild, Dawson, continue to keep me stabilized during the shaking of the foundations of my life. And my wife Susan, who so lovingly edits my feeble efforts at witnessing to the truth, is the light and hope of my life, as the dust is scattered to the four winds.

May you find a full measure of peace, hope and stability in these meditations on the Divine Mystery.

Lou Bauer

The most beautiful and deepest experience a man can have is the sense of the mysterious. It is the underlying principle of religion as well as of all serious endeavour in art and science. He who never had this experience seems to me is, if not dead, then at least blind. To sense that behind anything that can be experienced there is a something that our minds cannot grasp, whose beauty and sublimity reaches us only indirectly: this is religiousness. In this sense I am religious. To me it suffices to wonder at these secrets and to attempt humbly to grasp with my mind a mere image of the lofty structure of all there is.

Albert Einstein, 1932

Contents

Chapter 1
Lift Your Hearts on High

*H*ave you ever watched closely how some people walk? First there is the man who, standing erect, thrusts his chest proudly forward. He sends a message—I am confident.

Then there is the lady who slouches, drawing her shoulders into herself. She also sends a message—perhaps, I am fearful. There is the person who walks along, head hung low, staring at the ground as one foot is placed in front of the other. He too sends a message, but what is it?

Perhaps his posture betrays the weighty burdens of the life that he bears upon his shoulders. Or maybe he is trying to figure out where he is going, unsure of his direction, unable to trust where he is headed. Perhaps he is afraid of the future. Not knowing what to expect, he concentrates on every movement in the present moment. He is unable to anticipate, unable to be expectant. One thing is certain. He will see little and will miss much more. His world will be small and drab, composed of little more than toes! He is a person frightened by the future and afraid of what lies ahead. He is self-preoccupied. He is also alone. He sees no one else.

I suspect many people lead lives not unlike the man staring at the ground as he struggles ahead. I suspect even Jesus sensed that when he spoke in words that initially shock and jar us, especially when we hear them during the weeks of December, a time that is supposed to be the beginning of a season of joy and merriment. Jesus speaks of signs in the sun, moon, and stars, and we imagine nations suffering internal distress and people fainting with fear and foreboding about what is to come upon their personal worlds and upon their fragile lives.

There are two dimensions or manifestations of anxiety that imprison a person and cause the deepest pain in the soul. On the one hand, you are anxious about your daily life and its obligations, but you can usually manage these things if you act wisely with your meager resources.

But there is a deeper anxiety that gnaws at the edges of your soul and ruptures your hope for a night of refreshing and reinvigorating sleep. You are dying each day. The end is happening right beneath your nose. There is nothing subtle about this march to oblivion. Anxiety gnaws at your soul as the teeth go false and the knees and hips are replaced. So you bow your heavy head to avoid staring into the abyss of what is coming. It is too painful, and you will do everything in your power to seduce yourself into thinking otherwise, somehow believing that you can outlast what is on the horizon.

If, in your fearfulness, you dare not see what is coming, then perhaps you can *hear*. So Jesus offers you words that speak of an end. And not just an end, but a conclusion. He offers you an assurance of a reality that this world, this life, is ruled by another power, a power named love. When you allow yourself to hear what Jesus says about this love, his words awaken you from your slumber. These words of Jesus break into your life and they crack it wide open, like the egg shell shattering to yield new life.

"Look up!" he says. "Raise your head. Lift yourself from the dust of life. Behold, your redemption is drawing near!"

Redemption is coming? Oh, really? And who needs it? You mean me? Redeemed?

Yes, you! (And me, too.) Redeemed from our willfulness. Redeemed from our sin. Redeemed from our fixed gaze upon our every step, for we are lost and searching for direction. We are alone and unable to see others, curved in upon ourselves, about to trip and fall flat upon our faces.

"Look up!" Jesus says. "Behold, good things are coming." You and your world are being rescued from yourself. The God who made you, the God who loves you, is coming to rescue you. As you await that final coming in hope, it is enough for you simply to lift your head. To look from a new perspective that allows you to see things as they really are.

So lift your head! Lift it high! Strain your neck. Behold the Christ as he comes to be with you, to redeem you, to guide you safely home. He is leading you as he holds your hand, so look up for the Christ who is coming again.

Your redemption is *this moment* drawing near! Reach out your trembling hand and walk with the Good Shepherd, your head held high. Can you believe it?

Chapter 2
Holiness in Life's Desert

One of the earliest Christian writers, a man named Mark, begins his story this way: "The beginning of the good news of Jesus Christ, the Son of God." He then proceeds to tell the most outrageous and intriguing story about God that one could imagine. As the story begins, it is manifestly clear that his tale is counter-cultural, on a collision course with every human expectation about who God is and what it means to be religious. The world and what is real in it is about to be transformed, and the immediate question is: can this outrageous transformation happen to you and me? What may ensue if we yield to such a deity?

The almighty God makes a fresh appearance into the world. He steals in from the desert, like a sandstorm, in the person of a man burning with passion and simplicity: John the Baptizer.

Imagine that you are watching TV when suddenly the volume soars, and a voice is shouting at you, from a car dealer's lot, trying to get you to come down and make a deal on a sleek new automobile. Irritated by that shouting you reach for the remote to turn down the volume.

John the Baptizer, God's outrageous prophet, came on the airwaves of Palestine, screeching his call to prepare a way for the mystery of God. He is telling you to abandon all the old assumptions that have held your life together in a patchwork of band aids that barely conceal your woundedness. The almighty and mysterious power of love gets your attention by announcing world-transforming reality through a hermit from the desert, whose cholesterol-free diet was grasshoppers and wild honey. This is love, my friend, at its most exquisite beauty.

St. Mark calls it the *beginning* of the Good News of Jesus Christ, Son of God. This strange entry of the camel-coated Baptist is the fantastic beginning of God's love affair with the world, and it is an outrageous beginning with awesomely good news.

God's humble messenger begins the Gospel of Christ in the desert for a reason. The desert is a place of profound silence, interrupted only by the swooshing wind of a sandstorm. Life is harsh and fleeting in the desert. The desert yearns for water so that vegetation may flourish. God looks down upon human life and sees the desert, the wastelands we have created. He enters our deserts in the strange prophet John with buckets of water for cooling and refreshing baptism.

Into those corners of your life, deep inside where confusion, loneliness and fear seem so entrenched, God enters with his prophet's call to repent. He asks you to open the desert of your life to his life-giving waters, so that you may bloom and flourish and bear the fruits of abundant life. John shouts to you—a voice in your own private desert. Let go of all your failures! Relinquish all your anxious strivings! Come to the Jordan of baptism and be washed clean. Let your life be built on the strong foundation of this strange and wonderful love.

But remember: this isn't the end. This is only the beginning. This is the preparation for the emptiness of your life to be filled with God's tender mercy. Into the desert, the wild places of your life, God is sending his lowly ambassador of grace, John the Baptizer, with his invitation: "Prepare the way of the Lord, make his paths straight."

The road to Ouguiya, Burkina Faso in West Africa is a reasonably well-paved road with the usual potholes and herds of cattle crossing to slow the journey. The road from Ouguiya to the border town of Koro in Mali, West Africa is a badly deteriorated gravel road, and in the heat of a 100-degree afternoon, one's patience ebbs. But the road from Koro to Bankass—about twenty-five miles long and traveled at two in the afternoon—makes our drive something else. The road is nothing more than two deeply rutted tracks through the bush, created months ago by a truck trying to make it through in the rainy season. Now, in the dry season, the road is nearly impassable. But, wait. There are two tracks on the right...and two tracks on the left...each of them paralleling the rutted road. Which bypass do you take? Left or right? In this deserted place, the image floods your mind: "Prepare the way of the Lord...make his paths straight!"

You have been warned—these paths that seem like bypasses may veer off deep into the bush toward a remote village, at which point you will be lost in the wilderness. The choice becomes alarming when your sick wife speaks of a chill, a symptom of feared malaria, and your stomach churns from having eaten a bad omelet earlier that day. You take the path to the right, but it is not the right path because it does veer off, and you are nearly lost until you backtrack to the rutted path and take the left set of tracks.

You are so weary, and you long for a shepherd to lead you down paths of righteousness to still waters of safety and security.

Mark does an amazing thing with those ancient words, "make his paths straight." He changes one word of the text from Isaiah and uses a different word which means *to construct a new road.*

You are given a brand new path through the desert of life, an incredible new reality, which is life in Christ. This is God's outrageous new road to travel through life: the way of Christ and his passionate love and joy and carefree confidence.

What road are you traveling? Through what desert? There is a hermit named John who knows your desert and calls out to you now to prepare for a spectacular change. There is a strange moment that comes in the life of every religious person. It may happen when you are aging or when you are still youthful or somewhere in-between. Suddenly you realize that you are in the desert, alone and lost. You've done the religious thing all your life: worship, committees, prayer, soup kitchen, offerings. But now children are leaving, job is empty, parents are passing, exams have been failed, your lover has left you.

Don't be afraid of the desert. It is a holy place. John is there with you with his comforting promise: prepare the way of the Lord. If you are in the desert, it is because you are now learning to yearn for God alone, beyond all the tinsel and lights and gay wrapping paper, the dreams dashed, the sins committed, the failures known.

This is all true preparation for the next outrageous step of God, who will enter the manger of your heart with his Christ. God will cradle your heart in his arms. Yield in the desert and trust him. Trust him to bring you to still and shimmering waters.

"The beginning of the good news of Jesus Christ, the Son of God," begins today in your desert, as the camel-coated John, carrying his bag of grasshoppers, cries out to you: Prepare the way—yearn for God alone—he is coming to meet you in Bethlehem. Walk with outrageous, countercultural John . And know that God will come to you and dwell with you and be your God. Your empty life will bloom with his passion and grace.

Chapter 3
The Incomprehensible Mystery

*I*n Advent the adventure is now beginning. She kicks off the dust of the Judean hills as she hastens along the road. Something is pressing in. There is a profound urgency to her hurried steps. Is she frightened? Is she running from something? Or is she running to something? What is this little Jewish girl thinking about as she rushes along her lonely way to meet someone who, she prays, might understand her?

Fifteen years old—that's all. The manger scenes make her look so mature and maternal. But she was barely an adolescent, and adolescents are supposed to be preoccupied with themselves, asserting their independence and learning to negotiate the adult world. But someone told her God was growing something in her womb. Why was she suddenly running so fast? Was she frightened? Was she happy? Or just plain confused? Do you suppose that there was a measure of doubt and skepticism in this little girl's heart, and that was what sent her fleeing to the old woman, Elizabeth? (Is this what makes us flee the mystery this time of the year—its utter incomprehensibility?) Here she was, on the verge of having her marriage wrecked. Don't think this little child couldn't or didn't hurt. Could she turn to her parents? To her husband-to-be? What would she say? "An angel told me I am pregnant!" Sure, Mary. "God's Son is growing in my body!" Sure, Mary. Would anyone believe her? Could she even believe or trust herself? God is strange—God is mysterious—God is loving—but can this really be God's thing?

She could hardly get her little head around this mystery. Is it any easier for us to get our gray or balding heads around this mystery? Does the almighty and incomprehensible mystery of love, which is beyond anything we have ever known, really enter human life? Does infinite love entangle itself in human biology? Do divine attributes and genes intersperse themselves in this mysterious creature? Does God care that much about insignificant and sinful me to take such strange and humble highways into this broken world? The question haunts: of what worth am I to the mystery of the divine?

Mary knocks at the door—waiting. She waits, just as we have waited, since the day we could begin to talk until the cataracts overcome vision and the heart strains to beat out another moment of life. This feels like waiting an eternity...*for* eternity. Somehow, in the depths of her fragile juvenile heart,

6

she prays that it is true—that it's all true.

She is standing timidly, feeling more than a bit embarrassed. Suddenly, there in front of her is the old woman, the wrinkled old woman, Elizabeth, her belly bulging and sagging with joy. Her baby is doing summersaults of recognition, instant communication across time and space. Her womb vibrates with ecstasy as the Prophet, John, meets the Master, Jesus, and the holy story of the world's redemption begins to unfold. It is all happening, just as the angel promised!

And Mary gives birth to song: "My soul magnifies the Lord, and my spirit rejoices in God my Savior...He has exalted those of low degree...filled the hungry with good things and sent the rich away empty." This young girl now stands tall, filled with peace and serenity. Suddenly she has become a mature woman of profound faith. She has encountered the awesome mystery of God, before whom all creation trembles, and has opened her life to the unfolding power of God's love. She has become both a receptacle to and a vehicle of the magnetic grace that draws all things unto itself.

And little Mary, now safe and comfortable in Elizabeth's tent, stayed three months with this holy family, cherishing the great mystery of creation that she bore in her womb for you and for me.

The adventure is now beginning. Angels beckon you to trust the mystery now unfolding for you. They bid you to believe, with the profound simplicity of faith, what you have seen in the obedient Mary. They urge you to open your life to give birth to the grace and love that has redeemed this world and has made its home amongst those of low estate.

Come! Rejoice with Mary, Mother of our Lord, and Eternal Bearer of the Word. Great things are about to happen to those who wait in faith and simple trust.

Chapter 4
The Wooden Silence of Joseph

*H*e stands there, mute and silent, like the figure in the school nativity pageant. No one speaks to him. He says nothing. Nowhere in the entire New Testament does Joseph say anything. He speaks not a single a word. But in his apparent silence, he acts, and he acts in a most powerful way. His silent action unlocks, for all those who would look at him, the mystery of the faith. He's not jealous. Everyone wants to see her...to see him...the baby. He just stands there, wondering if anyone will ever understand him, wondering if anyone will ever see him as someone worthy to emulate.

Do you really understand what happened to Joseph? I think, perhaps, you do. Life was flowing so smoothly for him. The joyful moment was at hand, and once again he would experience the love and compassion of a woman. Once again he would know that strange beauty of sharing life with another person. And then, suddenly, it is all disrupted. Suddenly life is thrown into disarray. Suddenly what was beautiful about life looked ugly and shameful, as his dreams became grotesque nightmares. Life would never be the same again. Life, interrupted by fate, is shattered like a cheap mirror into lethal shards. That for which he had humbly dreamed and yearned was in shambles. The image of his first wife flashed before him. The ache for her love surged in his broken heart, but she had died and would never return to comfort him. He had hoped this would be the time for the young lass to revive his weary soul with her faithful care and loving touch. But now, it seemed, this was not to happen.

Have you yearned and dreamed of a sweet future? Have you been quite certain about how you wanted your life to turn out? Have you known that sudden and dramatic event that deals you, vulnerable and confused, the crushing blow? The sudden fracture that renders null and void all of your dreams? Joseph, in his silence, knew it well.

His woman was pregnant. The love of his life was bulging at the seams with a life that he knew not. Did he despair? Yes! Was he angry? Absolutely! And like anyone who has been the casualty of life's peculiar meanderings, he did what everyone does at such a moment. He agonized in his heart, bewildered by his options.

To be just is virtuous. To be compassionate is even more virtuous. Justice required that he divorce her, compassion that somehow he commute her sentence of lonely abandonment. He weighed the alternatives, pondered the outcome. Would the end justify the means? How could the greatest good be served? Like the ethicist in our profoundly confused culture, he wondered, "Would the cost outweigh the benefits?" He agonized in the silence of his heart. What do you suppose he concluded?

We will never know, because, in the middle of the night, God stole into Joseph's silent world. The divine touched him with the comforting words: "Do not be afraid Joseph."

God knows how frightened we are to be daring...to shock the world with simple faith.

Do not be afraid, Joseph, to take this woman as your wife. Because, dear Joseph, in the crisis of your life, God is working. In what looks like life's shambles, the sweetness of God can be tasted.

Justice was not enough. Compassion was not enough. Weighing all the alternatives was not enough. Only faith suffices when life is in upheaval.

Now Joseph stands silently at the manager. His silence can seem foreboding. Silence is often foreboding to mortals. But Joseph stands there in the silence of faith, the silence of trust, the silence of hope. The God who has given life will transform it into a beautiful thing. Only faith can make some sense of life's crises.

Can you allow Joseph to be your patron saint when you make your journey to Bethlehem? Like Joseph, can you bring with you, in the silence of your heart, all that troubles you? All that frightens you? All that makes you feel unworthy? Stand next to him as he confidently peers into the manger to behold the mystery of God. Let him share with you the hope that transformed his confused world into a peaceful place. Behold the trust that empowers him, through great danger and risk, to care for the Messiah, the hope of the world and the fulfillment of his life.

Perhaps you shiver in the cold tonight. But your heart can be warmed by this mysterious and awesome love of God. You can join me tonight at the stable, next to Joseph, silently beholding the wonder of God's love for us. See you in Bethlehem!

Chapter 5
Hope for the Hopeless

*A*n extraordinary number of men and women in countries throughout the world face off in battle lines every Christmas Eve as we celebrate the birth of the Prince of Peace. Each side is convinced that it knows the things that make for peace. Stubbornly self-reliant on their own resources, they stare at and taunt one another.

But nothing—not even these squabbles—can detract or divert our gaze from the enduring story and wonder at God's mysterious birth into the world in the babe of Bethlehem. In simple and silent ways, God reveals the things that make for peace, and the frantic and aggressive ways of the world are muted into silent wonder as the eternal power of love shapes and fashions the redemption of this aching world.

Why is it that we never tire of hearing read to us this brief little story of Jesus's birth? Why is it that churches split at the seams with overflow crowds? Why is it that city streets this night are bare? One day, during the week before Christmas, I set out to commune my congregation's shut-ins, knowing that in each home I would read the same lesson, *Luke 2*, the story of the Messiah's birth. Please forgive this humble pastor, but I pondered how bored I might be at the last reading. To my surprise, I found myself, each successive time, reading, with greater enthusiasm and wonder, this simple story of how your salvation and my salvation began.

What is the power of this story that grasps us so deeply? What is the power of this narrative that so enchants us?

It begins with this: for once we are listeners as God begins to speak his story of love. We sit and keep silence, as the only words that matter in the world are the symphony of the angels greeting the shepherds, inviting them to God's new-born nursery in Bethlehem, to coo and adore his new born son. God is the author—he in charge—writing the script that will eternally change the horizon of every future.

Only a God of profoundest love could have written a script that enters the muck and mire of a human stable, warmed by the breath of animals, on a frigid night. And you find that you are listening, listening down through all the years of your struggling and striving, and you know that you are at rest for once. Because there is a power of love in this world that is now in charge.

This is a power of love that knows where you have been coming from and where you want and need to go.

What is the power of this story of Jesus's birth? It is simply this: there is hope alive in this world, and this is a hope that cannot be shattered or broken.

Helmut Thielicke, a great German pastor and theologian, remarked one Christmas Eve, "Therefore Christmas will be first understood by those who have no more human hope."

Joseph was bereft of hope, a widower who knew what every human heart knows when someone we love is lost. Mary was bereft of hope, pregnant out of wedlock, damned by her elders and her religion, a teenager trapped. And the shepherds were hardly a cut above the criminals, eking out their existence like the homeless and the mentally ill. That's only the beginning of this precious story that unfolds through the lepers and cripples, the lonely and lost, the forgotten and despairing, the tax-collectors and outcasts, as God gathers up all of life in his infinite arms. Cradle and Cross are made of the same wood—symbols of the unbreakable hope of the child of Bethlehem and the Christ of the empty tomb who whispers continually to your sighing heart: I love you, you are precious to me, I love you dearly!

What enchants us in this story is that God *knows* what is like to live in this world as one of us. Life will be hard, even for God and his little child in this world, but he *knows*, and his word of love will be the last word as the world in silence listens. He brings hope with the gift of his grace. This hope is as sure as the rose blooms this night, out there in the memorial garden of your grief and sorrow and hopelessness.

Christmas assures you that God comes for *you*, no matter where you are, no matter who you are, no matter what you have done, no matter what you have left undone. And when everything is finished, when everything seems lost, that is when God's possibilities begin.

On Christmas night (and every night), may your old ways be finished. Let God's possibilities begin. The Christ is born! The rose is blooming! Hope is stirring, and love will triumph. There is peace...there will be peace! So sing the angels this holy night. Join your humble heart and grateful voice to their heavenly chorus, as heaven and earth now meet in Jesus, the new-born Christ.

Chapter 6
The Holy Story in a Dream

*W*hat if you lived your life according to your dreams? What do you suppose it would be like? Actually this isn't a fair question, is it? You are probably asking yourself, what does he mean by dreams? Does he mean those other worldly events that happen when I am safely tucked away in bed? Or does he mean by dreams my hopes and aspirations? What if he means both?

There is an often untold part of the Christmas story that I want to encourage you to ponder. It is the story of a dreamer whose life is profoundly transformed in his dreams. This story may be a revelation to you of how deeply and intimately God beckons to your soul to live the life of grace.

Joseph doesn't know it, but King Herod is frightened. He is threatened. Power, especially, illegitimate power, is often terrified, rendered helpless, by the birth of grace. So Herod decrees the slaughter of infants in a ruthless effort to silence grace—to end the life of the little Christ—and thus reorder the stability of his world. Wherever Christianity is truly vibrant, there is always deadly tension with the comfortable ordering of life!

In his weary sleep, deep in a dream, God speaks to Joseph: take your family and flee to Egypt. Joseph could have awakened and said, "No!" We might even have forgiven him for rejecting the nightmare—why should he live by a dream? Is this what happens to anyone who gets caught up with this Christ-child? Even you, who might dare to open your heart to the bizarre ways of God's meddling? Consider what has happened to this person named Joseph who opened himself to becoming the protector, the guardian, of God's dream for the world.

It was disruptive enough to make that trek to Bethlehem at the government's request. It was enough to watch his young bride writhing in labor, without midwife or relative to assist in delivery. To watch and help her give birth to a child whose legitimacy was still deeply in question. And then the dream. Or was it a nightmare? *Take your family and go to Africa!* An order to enter a strange land—a summons to pilgrimage. Leave home, Joseph. Leave everything familiar. Does Joseph dare? Do *you* dare to cherish the divine mystery in your life?

And so the birth of the Christ-child creates a refugee family, on the run in

12

the world at God's behest. Jesus enters the world as a refugee, following his father's dream. Never really at home in the world. Dislocated. The life of God's divine family begins in exile, homeless and in search of shelter. Should we ever be surprised by what happens to us...what awaits us...when we heed the dreams of God?

So the carpenter packs his treasures upon a mule and trudges across the dunes of the desert into a strange and alien future, a refugee in Egypt. Knowing no one in the strange land. No one to turn to for bread. No one to turn to for shelter. The carpenter, downsized to unemployment by God's strange dreams, takes odd jobs to keep the dream alive. Joseph, more than a survivor, is becoming a dreamer! Maybe we all have to go on pilgrimages into the unknown at the behest of our creator. Maybe the creator wants you to become a dreamer.

Sometime later, again in the depths of night, Joseph's sleep is disrupted by the one who calls the dreamer. The mystery is calling him out of exile and back home to Israel. Swiftly—decisively—he packs his divine treasures onto his mule, with all the excitement and anticipation which always accompanies the prospect of homecoming, to retrace his steps across the dunes.

But just as he approaches border control with Mary and Jesus, cuddled in her protective embrace on the donkey, something profound happens. Something that makes this one of the profoundest stories in the gospels. Joseph, standing there at the border and looking toward home, internalizes the dream. Because of the pilgrimage...because of exile...because of his reliance upon the grace of the mystery, he begins to live the dream himself!

Standing there at the border, yearning for his home in the world, Joseph makes the decision himself, *on his own* and out of fear for his child's life. Committed to cherishing the divine mystery, Joseph makes the decision NOT TO GO HOME to Judea, but to live in the obscurity and anonymity of a little burg called Nazareth, cherishing and caring for the mystery God entrusted to him—starting life all over again.

Those who go on God's pilgrimages, chasing His dreams, can never go home again, because, like Joseph, they learn to live and act in God's mystery. They have tasted the supreme joy of living with the mystery of God and cannot live otherwise in the world. And there is perhaps no greater and more instructive story for you for living life in the here and now, by grace, through faith, and on account of Christ, than this story about the dreaming carpenter, Joseph, and his refugee family.

I am convinced that God is speaking again to those who would dare to be dreamers. He is calling us to journey to Egypt, into exile, to cherish His mystery on behalf of His world. You don't have to be terribly perceptive to see the stirrings in our institutions, our groups, our churches, our personal lives: a hunger for meaning, a hunger for purpose, a hunger for love that we have not known before with this intensity. I sincerely believe these are the first signs that some are struggling to open their lives to holy pilgrimage in what has become a world now alien to LIFE.

If your nights are restless, and God has begun to speak to you in your dreams (whatever He means by dreams), you have begun to join all the refugees across time who have fled with the Holy Family on pilgrimage. God invites you now to journey to Egypt...into exile...but you, like Joseph and Mary, have nothing to fear if you hold the Christ Child tightly to your heart and step boldly into the journey...by grace, through faith, on account of the Christ Child. And as you travel, you will soon discover, like the Holy Family, that you have begun to live for yourself God's dream for the world.

Chapter 7
Dawn in the Sunset of Life

*Y*ou come to me and ask—it has happened many times before—"Pastor, how can I know the will of God?" I ponder silently and seemingly endlessly. You may think I have fallen asleep or into a trance. I labor painfully to give birth to an answer. Finally, words begin to form and I say to you then what I say to you now: Let me tell you a story!

There once was a man who lived in Mesopotamia—today it is the country of Iraq. This man was listening to the deeper pulses of his heartbeat, listening to that place inside himself we all know, where we hear a voice that often beckons to us to look at who we are and where we are. One day, as he listened deeply, a voice spoke to him: "Abraham, go from your country and your kindred and your father's house to the land I will show you."

The voice shattered the old man's calm repose. Did the voice know what he was asking? Didn't the voice have some sensitivity toward the plight of the elderly? After all, Abraham was 75 years old, his skin now leathery and wrinkling. Couldn't the voice leave this old man to pass his days in quiet retirement, rather than ask him to do what some young fool of a kid might do? And to leave his kinfolk? To abandon his country and pension and savings account? To leave the safety and heritage of his father's house?

Do you know what it was like to ask an old man from the ancient world to leave everything that was familiar to him—the *only* things that were familiar to him—to go on a journey when there were no such things as road maps? You know what sometimes happens to the aged when they are uprooted from their familiar surroundings—how disoriented they sometimes become. And this is the world before technology, when there were no signs to guide the way or announce the distance to the next city, no Google maps, no GPS. Life was family, and to ask one to leave family was to bid a man to go and die.

What weird, strange, and wondrous love enters a man's life at sunset and virtually bids him go and die? Do you think the God we worship is some kind granddaddy in the sky—or are you willing to allow God to be the powerful and dynamic force who creates the possible from the impossible—the new things out of that which is not? How easy it is to domesticate God to the point that we can no longer even hear the wild and passionate voice that bids us to take the risk of following the voice that speaks.

And how does the old man respond? Wouldn't it be nice to get inside the old man's head and hear him think out loud, wrestle with his doubts, catch a clue about what motivated him? Perhaps this might help us in our own struggles with that nagging voice. But the Bible is not interested in psychologizing or psychoanalyzing Abraham, because the Bible is simply not about that. The Bible doesn't want to go inside the old man's head to find out why he did what he did. It simply wants to hold out an image before us for you and me to learn from. The Bible simply says: *So Abraham went as the Lord had told him*, or, as the Book of Hebrews says: *He went out, not knowing where he was to go.*

He trusted the voice, and he obeyed. That is all the Bible wants us to catch sight of. It is all that ever matters, when dealing with this wild and passionate love of God. He trusted and obeyed. You know, you could sum up everything that is the Christian faith in those few words: he trusted and obeyed.

He gathered up his wife Sarah, his brother's son, Lot, some of his servants, his sleeping bags, canteens, pots and pans, tents and clothes, spices and medicines, clothes hangers and towels and everything else he had accumulated in the attic in the past 75 years—and he trusted—he obeyed—he went forth. South, as a matter of fact, wandering without a road map or GPS, going somewhere in the sunset of his life in search of the sunrise.

There were no McDonalds or Burger Kings on the way—not even a Holiday Inn. Nothing but empty and dry space, hostile tribes, and a blazing sun as they lurched forward in old age, doing what children might be doing. Trusting, obeying, and going forth. But they weren't left alone, because the wild and passionate love of God asks no one to journey through life alone. God appears along the way and greets them when, huffing and puffing and dragging along their arthritic frames, they reach the promised land. God never asks one to follow without the assurance that, though hidden, he goes with us.

You can read the rest of the story about this man of faith (the author of the Bible would be delighted if you did), because this whole story of Abraham is told to give you a reliable picture of what it means for you, in your life, to have faith and to be obedient. In fact, the Bible even invites you to be an Abraham: to listen, to trust, to obey, and then to go forth confidently.

There is a New Testament model of Abraham. One who listened in the wilderness, one who trusted the voice he heard, one who obeyed, and one who went forth. His name is Jesus. So trusting and determined is he to follow, to obey, that he would not even allow death to interfere with his journey. That's the kind of confident courage and profound trust with which you and I are invited to live our journey.

Still we ask, "How can I know the will of God?" The answer is that we can't know—at least not with certainty of detail. God does not provide a roadmap, carefully marked out for us (in fact, it seems that he is making it up along the way). God simply invites us to live by faith, that is, with trust in the one who calls, and perhaps with a measure of prayer, as in the beautiful prayer found in the Order for Evening Prayer in the Lutheran Book of Worship:

Lord God, you have called your servants to ventures of which we cannot see the end, by paths as yet untrodden, through perils unknown. Give us faith to go out with good courage, not knowing where we go, but only that your hand is leading us and your love is supporting us, through Jesus Christ our Lord.

Chapter 8
The Master Cried

*T*he story begins in an all too familiar way: *Now a certain man was ill.* Those words can be a chilling reminder of mortality and the limits of life. Now a certain man was ill. You surely know, or have known, someone who was ill. Ill in that deeper way which some describe clinically as "terminal." You already have a hint about where this story is going. Those words touch the essence of what we know about life, a reality from which we so often shrink: we are vulnerable. Death waits silently and patiently for its opportune moment. It takes only a few brief and seemingly innocuous words to remind us of the common denominator of our experience that seems to bind us together as human beings. Was it a tumorous cancer that had laid him low, or liver failure, or a stroke, or old age? Maybe pneumonia or even the flu was sapping his strength and robbing him of his life.

All Mary and Martha knew was that their brother was gravely ill, and so they turned, as we so often do, to a trusted friend with the brief but fateful message: "Lord, he whom you love is ill." It is a jarring message to receive— that someone who has delighted your life is now suffering and vulnerable. Seldom do we hear anywhere else of such a profoundly intimate relationship as the one between Jesus and Lazarus. There was a special place in Jesus's heart for this man. He had probably spent so many evenings in Lazarus's home, sharing friendship and laughter with him and his sisters—no longer a guest, but now part of the family.

You know that Jesus seemed always to have a special place in his heart for those who were suffering and those at the edge of life's great abyss. It seems that the most appropriate way for us to pray for others' healing would be to speak the words of Mary and Martha: "Lord, the one whom you love is ill."

When Jesus first heard those ominous words, he announced that this was not illness unto death. Rather, it was the initial foray in God's glorification. But lest you think that God goes around striking down the strong, so that his son will have another opportunity to show off, remember that, for the Gospel writer, John, the glorification of God comes when Jesus encounters the reality of his own death. Then John reminds us that Jesus loved Martha, Mary, and Lazarus. John seems to widen the circle of those whom Jesus loved, as if to suggest that this whole story may include you and me as Lazaruses and Marys and Marthas—people whom he loves deeply and wondrously.

For some reason, Jesus lingered for two days without responding to the sisters' plea, plus another day for the journey itself. Is that any way to treat friends, especially someone you allegedly love? Would you have dawdled in the face of that news? Why did he linger? No one knows really. On the one hand, as difficult as his delay may be to understand, it may point to a most wondrous and mysterious love that exceeds our comprehension. This is a love that moves at its own time and own pace, a love supremely confident of something few us comprehend: the assurance that death can be laughed at.

On the other hand, perhaps Jesus is caught in a profound struggle between the fear of returning to this hostile territory and his love for a friend. Perhaps he agonizes those two days, remembering that he had said, "No greater love hath a man than to lay down his life for a friend." Sometimes grief, deep grief, delays us, slows us down, and renders us inert.

Whatever his reason, finally he returns to the stench of death. And Martha, in her grief, rushes to meet him and twists the knife of guilt: "Lord if you had been here, my brother would not have died." Grief makes us say things like this. She was angry. He had dawdled. She was helpless. Surely there was something she could have done—something he could have done. Someday she might accept her brother's death—but not yet. If only they had beckoned a physician, a healer, when there was still time. And even Mary, voicing the exact same words, struggles to cope with her helplessness in the face of human vulnerability. "If you had been here, Lord, my brother would not have died."

The Gospel writer, John, tells us that Jesus, upon seeing Mary weeping and hearing these words, was deeply moved in spirit and troubled. Those are soft words for what was Jesus's own gut-wrenching grief at his friend's death. He had feelings, too, and he was shaken to the depth of his soul and numbed by loss. Then Jesus, following Mary, went to the tomb. And John says, "He wept!" He broke down and cried like a little child.

Men—don't be afraid to cry. Your Lord wept. God sheds tears of grief and love for what he sees in you and me—the reality of our vulnerability. God weeps for us. God cries out in grief and sorrow at our brokenness, something his compassion can no longer bear. This love at the heart of creation, at the heart of the universe, aches for us to live and share life with him.

Jesus lifts his head and whispers, "Abba...Father." The scene prefigures Gethsemane, for he knows that calling Lazarus out of the tomb means that he must enter it. And then he cried with a loud voice—no, he roared at the top of his lungs, beyond the abyss that separates us from life (and across which he would soon whisper, in his last gasp, "It is finished."). He roared, "Lazarus, come out!" And that greatest of loves began, in that moment, to lay down his life for all of us, his friends.

This was no cruel April Fool's joke. The dead man came out, his hands and feet bound with bandages and his face wrapped with a cloth. Jesus said to them: "Unbind him, and let him go." Unbind us Lord...and let us go. Release us from the chasm of our broken, empty lives.

Eugene O'Neill called his last play, *Lazarus Laughed*. It is the story of a lover of Jesus who had tasted death and seen it for what it is. He emerges from the tomb and shouts: Laugh with me! Death is dead! Fear is no more! There is only life! There is only laughter!

Chapter 9
Care for My Boys, Please

*H*ave you ever travelled in a foreign country where you have felt uneasy about yourself and all your possessions? You have this eerie feeling that everything you have is in danger of being taken from you—your luggage, your passport, your credit cards, your cell phone. Should you lose your passport, no one would know who you are. Suddenly, you might be no one. Believe me, I know this fear, and I am sure you can imagine it if you have not felt it, too. It is frightening! Suppose today that happened to you in Beirut or Cairo or Damascus.

There is something in all of us that struggles for survival. It runs deep in our biology—so deep that we have little, if any, control over it. When something threatens you, perhaps threatens your very existence, a deep instinct begins to assert itself—to preserve you and to keep you alive, no matter what the cost. Ethics and morality seem to ebb at this moment. What matters is self-survival. Without knowing what happened, you find yourself entangled in a nasty, brutish world of me-first people, competing to preserve their turf. And life along with it. Some strange and ugly things can happen when you are living down there at the survival level.

A mother came to Jesus and asked the question that any mother might ask: "I want something from you, Jesus. Take care of my children. I have two boys. I love them dearly, Jesus. I raised them...sweated through the long nights with them. I know the pains of labor. Jesus, take care of them. Assure me that they will be with you, no matter what happens—one at your right hand and one at your left hand in your kingdom."

She had heard rumors and rumblings, and she knew that there was deep danger at hand. She knew that she was wandering in a strange and alien land where more than possessions mattered; even life itself was now at stake. She was a mother, and even her survival was at stake. Only her children would ever take care of her. And so she dared...she dared to ask the ultimate question.

You have to admire her—even though she was so deeply confused, as you and I are so often confused. To your dismay (because this isn't who you thought you were), you find yourself elbowing, with all your might, to secure for yourself a place of ultimate worth. You don't even see the faces of those you are shoving aside.

She wants to protect her children, this mother of the Zebedees. She wants to protect herself. Each of us, down deep inside, wants to preserve our personal integrity. Because we are not always so sure that there is another who will do so. At least not ultimately.

And so she brusquely demands, within earshot of everyone, "Command, Jesus!" Not a gentle request, but a blatant demand! "Command, Lord, that my boys will be right there with you when you make it big!" Save us, Jesus. To hell with the rest of humanity, Jesus. Take care of me and my boys.

She's a rather pathetic creature, isn't she? Shameful, really. We avert our eyes. No one else matters...me...me...me! What's at her center? Me...me...me. It's sad, and a little embarrassing to watch this frightened woman, like an infant, crying out to the universe, demanding attention. It's distressing that anyone should ever be so frightened, frightened by life or by death. It's so stunting and constricting to live entombed by that kind of fear. Look at what fear does to this woman. Can you see what fear does to life? To your life?

Jesus's reply to her is not what she expected—I wonder if she even heard it. He replies, "I can't do that—it's not that way. God is at the center—not me." He calls his disciples aside and tells them, "Start practicing right now for what is yet to come. Whoever would be great among you—become a servant!" Take second place. And Jesus proceeds to pick up his cross and march to Jerusalem to show everyone what it means to forget about yourself and your survival, to gain everything. He shows you what it means to live life in faith, rather than tremble your way through your days in fear.

There is only one reason why Jesus was able to live life so free from fear—so selflessly, compassionately, and passionately. He was God-centered, rather than self-centered. He trusted that his dear Father—his Abba—had a place prepared for him at the end of this short road to Jerusalem. That is why he could march through the dust....at peace, confident, forgiving his way down through the fears unleashed upon him.

A crow once flew into the sky
with a piece of meat in its beak.
Twenty crows set out in pursuit
of it and attacked it vigorously.

The crow finally let the piece of
meat drop. Its pursuers then

left it alone and flew shrieking
after the morsel.

Said the crow, "I've lost the meat,
and gained this peaceful sky."

Jesus said, "I go to prepare a place for you, that where I am, you may be also." Do you believe that? With your trembling heart, do you trust him?

Chapter 10
A Child is Lost

*A*ngry storm clouds are gathering above the Jerusalem sky, like a council of war about to unleash its final fury. The afternoon sky is streaked with that sickening yellow that portends a violent eruption of nature. Even nature knows that this is a day unlike any the world has seen before, and like none that it will ever see again. The world's redemption drawing nigh.

Then a silence—not an empty silence, but a roaring silence, deeper than any silence ever known—seizes the city. Fathers and mothers frantically call to their playful children. "Abraham, come inside." "Miriam, hurry home, you'll get drenched." "Saul come here!" And the children gather their stick figures and dolls and rush to the safety of their parents' arms, as the thunder cracks and lightning streaks across the sky, illuminating this darkest hour. All are safely home...but one!

A child is lost, somewhere outside the city wall. Lost on a hill. Lost and weeping in terror that he will never find his way home again. Where is his Father? Can't he find him? Can't he reach out and embrace him, lead him safely home to comfort him and anoint his wounds? Hidden and muffled beneath the thunder, a weeping voice from heaven cries out: Jesus, Jesus, my beloved son, Where are you? Come in from the storm—it will destroy you.

The child of Bethlehem is lost in Jerusalem. He who played with hammers and nails at the feet of Joseph the Carpenter, hangs now himself, nailed through hands and feet to a tree. He who welcomed children with his winsome smile, arms open to embrace them with his Father's love, is now a lost child searching the skies for even the hint of compassion as his blood drips and puddles on Golgotha. Is life so loveless to the lost and dying? And he who called to the heavens time and again in joyful communion, "Abba, Father, my Dear One," uniting the heavens and earth so severed since Eden, now scans the earth at his feet for his Father's searching footsteps.

But the child is lost and cannot find his way home. No hand of a strong Father into which to place his own trembling hand. Then the frightened cry from the cross as the burden of the world's suffering crushes upon his shoulders: "My God, My God, Why have you forsaken me?" Even the halls of heaven are shattered by the cry of this lost and dying child. God calling to God across the vast depths of space—the weeping Father absorbing into his

24

heart the ache of losing his only Son.

This dreadful moment of rupture in heaven and earth echoes the cry of everyone across the ages and millennia who have lost their way and wonder if anyone, anything in all creation cares. The cry from the emergency room. The cry from the sick bed. The cry of unrelieved sin from the confessional. The cry from the shattered relationship. The cry of the heart from failure. The cry from the beloved's tomb. We depend upon the dependable, but for a chilling moment everyone enters the Godless abyss of the lost child, where not even a God shouted at seems to hear the lost lamb's bleating of abandonment.

Now, it is important, for you who have known the forsakenness of the lost child of the cross, to listen attentively to the dying Master, as if your existence depended upon him. Because it does. As life seeps from the wounds of his precious body, in a final act of glory he turns his head to heaven and whispers, "Father...Father...Father...into your hands I commend my spirit."

The lost child still trusts! He can still trust his Father will find him, receive him, and bring him safely home. All evidence to the contrary—with no sign whatsoever that anyone or anything cares—Jesus reveals the ultimate human moment of triumph: to live in faith and die in trust. The lost child of the cross, in his last act of obedient trust, becomes the bridge across which all we who have lost our way in life can journey into our Father's waiting arms.

And in the next moment, when time yields to eternity and space dissolves into the heavens, the lost child of the cross falls into the arms of his waiting Father, his weeping Father, who rejoices that his only Son has found and revealed the way home through the absolute darkness of night. Our Father lifts him up, as the dawning sun rises, to heal his wounds, to welcome him and all his friends into the halls of heaven, where lilies bloom eternally and angels prepare the tables, placing the napkins for the heavenly feast of joy. "Rejoice with me," weeps the Father in joy, "for this son of mine was dead and is alive again—he was lost and is found!"

And because the Child of Bethlehem became lost for our sakes and found the way home through the cross, no one—none of us—need ever fear the forsakenness of God. Because of the Crucified One, we can live in faith and die in trust!

Chapter 11
The Captain Has Won

She stood there with the other women—but at a distance. How else could you stand there at a crucifixion, other than at a distance? The sight is ghastly, the suffering unbearable, the pain intense, the shame heart-wrenching. She stood at a distance from his cross, perplexed. This man had intrigued her—she had valued his friendship. Somehow, he was so unique: his way with people, his compassion and understanding, his sensitivity and grace, his patience and forbearance. Simply to be in his presence brought healing to frightened and broken hearts.

The mother of the sons of Zebedee kept her distance, pondering. So this was the cup he was to drink. That's what he had said when she asked him to look out for her boys. "Are you able to drink the cup I am to drink?" And now there he hangs, not just sipping the cup but drenched in its agony and defeat. Why does the world destroy what is brightest and best? Why does the world reject what is purest and holiest? What is that power of evil in the human heart, so deeply hidden that it masquerades as justice and righteousness? Why does that power of evil lift its hand to strike another human being? For what does the human heart rage in such outrageous and senseless anger?

Answers will not be given to this woman's questing heart as she watches her friend lurch into death on his cross. She will have to wait to see that God has a hand in all of this, a hand that is like a heart absorbing every blow and twitch of nerve in pain. That heart—God's heart—loves, and that heart knows that the only way to defeat death, the only way to defeat the rage and anger in humankind, is through a suffering, dying love. Only love, my friend, only patient, long-suffering love can overcome evil.

The man who is hanging there for us, so that we will never have to hang there, knew that. He came from his Father's bosom, bursting with compassion and tenderness, and now he was returning to his Father's loving arms, forgiving every sinner along the way who would reach out to him and dare to implore him, "Please, take me with you!"

Angels are watching over him. They have been, ever since they sang his birth with cosmic joy. They keep their lonely vigil, praying for him, as he gathers upon his shoulders the infinite burden of all the sin that has ever been and ever will be, absorbing it into his own body and overcoming it with the love that cannot be broken. Not with nails, not with thorns, not with crosses.

They spit at Jesus—they spit at God—but he won't stop now what he has begun, because that face of love, covered with spit, can still forgive and can still, in its infinitely unfathomable depth, embrace rejection.

While Mother Zebedee is perplexed, the angels are awed by this sight. No sin will ever be unforgiven. Nothing can stop now what has begun on that bloody hill outside Jerusalem.

The angels can see now what this woman could not notice. That even in these dark moments the world is tilting. No longer just hurtling madly through space, but tilting home toward paradise. Like a mast on a mighty ship, his blood-stained body is spread out like a sail gathering the wind. His dying life is turning the world onto a new course: homeward, to safe harbor, to be eternally anchored in his Father's arms.

There will be a moment soon when he breathes his last and all will seem like a ship lost in the night, lost in the eternal night of darkness, sinking deep into the cold abyss. But the angels will not flinch. They will stand there, waiting with their ropes and halyards in hand, knowing that the blood-red sail will come home in a few days glistening white. The ship will be heavy with a full cargo of humanity, and the angels will be singing hymns of praise and thanksgiving that the journey is over. No more storms. No more raging winds or souls. Simply peace, silent peace, gentle winds blowing, and the masthead now anchored on shore as God's eternal trophy of love that endured and conquered. The captain has completed his mission!

We can linger at a distance from the cross, as perplexed as the mother of the sons of Zebedee, keeping our distance from this awful sight. Or we can stand with the angels amidst that peace which has begun to blow its winds gently out of Jerusalem to all parts of the earth, through every moment in time. We can quietly whisper to ourselves—or shout to world: the captain has won!

Chapter 12
Thirsting for Human Souls

*A*bandoned in the midst of life's lonely desert, his parched throat wails in yearning: *I thirst*! Dehydration now seizes his precious body and drains life's last fluids from his tender soul. Dust swirls and envelops his cross on this darkened Friday—only heavy clouds moistened with his Father's tears, now beckon him home into greener pastures, into his Father's arms.

As the waters of life gush from his body onto the dusty earth of Golgotha, he scans the horizon for a friendly face and cries out for the most basic sign of human compassion: "I thirst!" Is there not some kind person who will moisten his parched and thirsty soul? Is there not someone willing to ease the pain in the final moments of the body's desiccation? Someone takes a sponge, wets it with vinegar, and thrusts its bitter sourness to his sweet lips. This was the world's last offering to its dying savior! Humanity carelessly brushing the lips of its God with vinegar.

This is he who had showered parched and empty lives with his refreshing grace and love...he who had washed the eyes of the blind with his own saliva...he who had plunged headlong into the Jordan stream, staggering through the mud to his Father's delight...he who had begged a woman at a well for a small cup of water...he who had commended the saints, "I was thirsty and you gave me drink"...he whose life was the epitome of the blessed one who hungered and thirsted for righteousness in every cell of his body. And the world's last offering to its dying savior was a sponge soaked with sour vinegar to quench his ravishing thirst.

But perhaps, just perhaps, that last plaintive cry for water was a proud announcement of his mission to the world. "I thirst," he cries out. I thirst for human souls to come to me so that I may lift them up and take them home. I yearn for human hearts—broken hearts, frightened hearts, weary hearts, weakened hearts, grieving hearts—to come to me, so I may satisfy their yearning. Come to me, and I will give you drink. Come to me, and I will bathe you with the waters of eternity. Even in his dying moments, in unquenchable love, he turns to a dying comrade, quenching his thirst with the refreshing waters of eternity, "Today, you will be with me in paradise." Now all who walk through the ultimate desert of life do not walk alone. They walk next to the shepherd who knows the way to lush and verdant pastures.

But now the cross has wrought its end, and the Great Shepherd, the Lamb of God, goes forth, leading his sheep home to his Father's arms. The dust-laden air of Golgotha, polluted with death, gives way before the rising shepherd. Green pastures and still waters begin to come into focus as the fresh airs of eternity waft gently around his scarred and sacred body. Angels greet him in his holy ascent, their rods and their staffs comforting him. Heavenly choirs sing in welcome to the Lamb of God who thirsts for the souls of the world. Fragrant lilies bow in reverence to kiss his dusty feet in greeting, as he and his lambs pass triumphantly by. Off in the distance, the Father waits—his arms spanning eternity—to embrace His beloved Son and greet his flock for whom he died.

He has gone home now, the great shepherd of the sheep, inviting all who thirst for life to follow his sacred way into eternity. Because he lives, our cups runneth over, the pastures are green and lush, abundant with fountains and pools of refreshing water, and goodness and mercy shall follow us all the days of our lives.

And yet he comes to us—thirsting, thirsting. What will you offer him to quench his thirst? A sponge soured with vinegar? Why not offer him—your soul!

Chapter 13
It is Finished

*I*t is now deep into the stench of that afternoon. The angry mob has gone to their homes to celebrate the holy Sabbath, satisfied that the world has again been put right by a lynching. Only the innocent victim remains on the hill, impaled upon a cross, his loneliness deepening now with only his mother, his brother and a few soldiers at hand. The silence, the silence when death approaches, is broken only by the tears of a mother as they strike the earth and are absorbed into the dust.

The lover of the world now hangs his thorn-crowned head, his precious blood now mingled on the ground with his mother's tears. The end is near...or is it the beginning? One beautiful life, lived with such astounding confidence in life's goodness. One life, lived with such astounding confidence that God embraced him every moment. One life, lived in such unshakeable trust that death is not the end. Such a life, now ending at the hands of human envy...and fear. *Our* envy...*our* fear!

It all sounds like such a horrendous defeat for God on that Judean hill. Never underestimate the power of human envy and fear. It can bring God to his knees...or nail him to a cross. But the silence is pierced as the afternoon ends with a cry of victory...a roar of triumph: "It is finished!" Here, in the darkest moment of human history, a choir of angels echoes from the halls of heaven in mighty choral refrain: "It is finished—it is finished."

But *what* was finished, when so much in this world, so much in life, seems unfinished? What had the carpenter of Nazareth finished on his cross? Dare we ask, "What, Lord, has been finished?"

As dark as it is, this dreadful afternoon on Golgotha, try to cast your mind back a few months to another dark evening. An evening when the very stars sizzle with excitement. It is Christmas Eve. Lives are merry. Children squirm with excitement. In an evergreen scented church, the lesson is read from the Gospel of John—the same Gospel from which dying Jesus cries out in triumph: "It is finished!'

The lector reads the words of Jesus's life begun in our midst: *In the beginning was the Word, and the Word was with God, and the Word was God...and the Word became flesh and dwelt amongst us.* Eventually the lector concludes, *No one has ever seen God. It is God the only Son who is close to the Father's heart, who has made him known.* And the congregation sings in holy chant, "Of the Father's Love Begotten."

It is the Father's heart that has been laid bare in the life and death of this carpenter from Nazareth. It is the Father's heart that has been laid bare on the cross, on a Friday that we must ultimately call "Good." We have seen God, if we have beheld the stunning life and sacred death of Jesus, the Jewish carpenter of Nazareth. For on this cross, God has made a sacrifice to us.

No more bulls and rams slaughtered at the altar by the priests. No more cereal offerings to the Holy One. No more tithes. No more good acts. No more just deeds. No more committee meetings offered up in sacrifice to the Holy One we fear.

All that is finished, for the Father, in his love, has made sacrifice to us in his only child who slips toward death on the sacrificial cross. It is finished, for the heart of our Father has been revealed. We have seen God as his love bursts forth from that cross to embrace us. This is God's sacrifice of himself, so that we may live boldly and die gracefully. The cry of victory reverberates across time and space, filling the creation: "IT IS FINISHED." What was begun in the Garden of Eden will now be accomplished in the garden tomb.

And the carpenter of Nazareth bowed his head, breathed his last, and gave up his spirit. The victorious Prince of Peace goes forth now to prepare the place for us in his Father's heart. His blood red banners stream afar, as he gathers up in his bosom all lost souls who have gone before us. There is my mother...there is my father...and there, in his bosom, I will go. His blood red banners of victory stream afar, as he gathers up your lost soul in his bosom and bears you home. His blood red banners stream afar, as he gathers up all the lost souls who come after us, bearing us all home in his bosom...to our Father.

Angels chant their hearts out in the halls of heaven amidst the scent of evergreen and everlasting lilies. The Victor is home, bearing all those treasured souls in his bosom, spreading them out in triumph before the Father. "Father, it is finished! It is finished." It has begun!

Chapter 14
Jesus, Remember Me

*H*e hangs there that final Friday morning on a cross, the last measure of life draining from his limp and pain-racked body. He has no name by which we remember him—no one stands at the foot of his cross to mourn his passing. He dies in utter loneliness. No tears wet the ground as this stranger on the cross is swept away into the sea of history, about to be forgotten. We know only that he was a thief, now crushed beneath the weight of the state's yearning for law and order. Had he stolen food to feed his family? Had he swindled a tax-collector? Had he lifted a lamb from a neighbor's flock? Had his politics urged him to yearn for a new day for his oppressed nation? Or was he simply a social misfit? Who knows?

It doesn't matter at this moment, as his last gasps for breath signal the approach of his lonely end. Next to him hangs another, a crown of thorns piercing his skull. Even in his innocent suffering, his pain-filled face radiates compassion. There is something about this man, even in his profound woundedness, even in his helpless weakness, that signals strength and purpose. Even now, in this horrible moment, looking into his emptying eyes, one can see the last flicker of love, inviting the thief to leave his loneliness and enter the fellowship of suffering love: Come to me all you who are heavily burdened, and I will give you rest.

In the single, most decisive moment of his life, when there were but a few moments left, the thief turns to the dying king and pleads, "Jesus, remember me when you come into your kingdom."

Jesus, remember me! Like a lost child calling for Mother, "Do not forget me!" On behalf of the whole creation in its woundedness, and for the whole human race in its loneliness, the thief cries out not to be forgotten. Just as, even now, you sigh from the hidden depths of your heart: Remember me!

Turning his thorn-crowned head to the pleading man, the master of grace answers, eternally, the lonely cry of all humanity who would turn toward him: Truly, truly, my brother, my sister, today you will be with me in paradise. All tears wiped away. No more sorrow. No more hunger. No more self-hatred. No more guilt. No more woundedness. No more loneliness. Enter into the halls of paradise in the fellowship of the blessed, those whom you have loved and who have loved you.

And now the wounded healer, the dying Son of God, begins his journey home. His crimson banner streams through the air, as he bears his trophy into the halls of paradise. The lilies bow in reverence to him. The angels' wings flutter in joy and anticipation. In his arms he bears one wounded soul, now made whole! One wounded thief restored, beginning the great and endless procession to wholeness of those who have fallen before and those who have yet to follow—all of those who, in their brokenness, turn to the wounded healer and simply ask: "Remember me! Remember me!"

From afar the Father runs out through the stars to embrace his Son. The Son is home at last, bringing with him the endless procession of wounded brothers and sisters who have had the courage to pray: "Remember me!" You, too, have known woundedness. You know how badly broken you are. But the day of salvation is drawing near. Turn to the cross and simply beg: "Jesus, remember me, when you come into your kingdom!"

Chapter 15
I Am Truth!

Michael Kaunga was a fourth year seminary student at Paulinum Lutheran Seminary in the African nation of Namibia. His greatest dream, after four years of study, was about to become true—he would soon be ordained as a Lutheran pastor. Michael was an extraordinarily engaging person with many intellectual gifts and a smile that melted the hearts of all of us who worked with and taught him.

Michael Kaunga was a faculty favorite—he was about to graduate with a diploma with "Distinction in Greek." He had mastered biblical Greek as few other students had, and his keen interest and understanding of the New Testament deeply impressed his faculty mentors. Michael was what has been so desperately needed in seminaries and divinity schools on the African continent: a true African who could go on to get his doctorate in New Testament and return to teach his comrades the church's witness to the truth.

One day Michael stopped by our flat, as he often did, to ask Susan to correct his English and seek advice from me on a theological assignment. But on this day his engaging smile was replaced by wrinkled pain upon his face. "Tatekulu Bauer and Meme Susan," he whispered, "I must discuss something with you!" His voice a mere whisper, he said, "I have been having chest pains the past two years. I went to the hospital in Katutura and they gave me a prescription for ibuprofen and a handful of vitamins. But my pains have persisted. I went to a witch doctor in the North (*traditional healer* is the Politically Correct term for witch doctor—75% of highly professional Namibians have sought medical help from a witch doctor.). But he did not help."

"Then I went to a witch doctor here in Windhoek. I had to stand in line for over two hours. She took me into her office and told me to lie down on a table. Then she put her hand on my chest like a fist. Then she began pulling things from my chest and throwing what she took from my chest onto the floor." Then the smile returned to Michael's face. "I just don't know," he said. "She pulled out what looked like a piece of pantyhose...some pebbles and stones...some small sticks...pieces of newspaper. I just don't know, Tatekulu and Meme, "What is the truth?"

Michael's confusion about what to believe—what is true?—is there a dependable truth?—is a parable for today and for all of us, and his question is global, because earth and all her creatures now reel in confusion. Is there a truth beyond my own personal beliefs, dark opinions and feeble reasoning? Is there a truth that engages me, shapes me, shows me how to live? Is there a truth that I can confidently announce to all, "This is the truth!" Is there truth beyond what Pope Benedict XVI recently identified as the "dictatorship of relativism?" Namely, is there something more than the debilitating confusion of my opinion versus your opinion, my truth versus your truth? Surely there must be a truth beyond all the sinful hidden human agendas that manipulate our fears through the seductive powers of persuasion.

You will recall, of course, that some 2000 years ago, at the trial of the Carpenter of Nazareth, Pilate asked, (whether sarcastically or in pained honesty, we do not know), this global question, "What, my friend, is truth?" *And the Carpenter of Nazareth stood there silently!* The Carpenter of Nazareth still stands before us, in the face of modernity and post-modernity's moral, ethical and intellectual chaos, waiting for the world, on its confused axis, to turn toward him.

Earlier, when Jesus is bidding farewell to those few followers who had glimpsed something of the truth in him, Thomas poses the urgent question for all of us from his anxious and confused heart: how can we know the truthful way? Sometimes I think that Thomas was the great intellect amongst the disciples—a most thoughtful one who, like us, yearned for the truth in the midst of his doubts. And this humble Carpenter of Nazareth replied to his friend, and for all the world to hear, "I am the way...the truth...the life." Or shall we translate literally his words: "I am truth...I am life!"

With Athens in shambles and Rome deteriorating, Jerusalem beckons the world to behold in this humble carpenter the truth of existence...the truth of reality. He is the one to whom we pray, for his compassion, for his courage, for his identification with the poor and the oppressed, for his obedience to his Father's truth, for his habit of living simply and possessing little, for his embrace of all who suffer or who have lost their way, for his vision for this fallen word's redemption and reconciliation, and for his delight in the beauty and sacredness of this creation.

Enable us always to receive him—the truth and the life—with thanksgiving, and to conform our lives to his. To conform every shred of our daily existence to Christ and his cross, the living truth of the cosmos.

When Jesus, truth and life, bade his final farewell to his friends, he said to them, "As the Father has sent me, so I send you." I send you to our brothers and sisters in El Salvador. I send you to our sisters and brothers in Africa. I send you to our sisters and brothers in Belarus. I send you to your brothers and sisters, your children, your spouse...to reveal the truth and ultimate mystery of life.

May you also respond to the Carpenter of Nazareth, standing before you today, with the confession of Thomas as he stared into the eyes and the wounds of living truth: "My Lord and my God!"

Chapter 16
The Light of Life in Death's Darkness

*I*t was still dark, not quite dawn, according to Matthew, who seems to suggest a deeper darkness than the fading cover of night. Mary Magdalene and the other Mary grope through this darkness toward the grave of their friend. But it was more than the heavy darkness of the night through which they were groping—it was the darkness of life's finality. They were going simply to see his sepulcher. They knew what to expect down at the end of that path. A tomb. A marker. A stone. A dead friend.

Can you blame them for being so downright realistic? Can you blame them for being so downright honest? Everything in life, everything in their experience, had taught them what to expect: at the end of the path lies death, shielded by a tomb. Can you blame them for having perceived so little about reality?

How about you? Do you expect to find anything other than what they expected to find? Come now, really, do you have the smallest hunch that you just might encounter a living Lord? Perhaps you have a faint glimmer of hope that, with an adjustment of your life, an adjustment of your heart, or an adjustment your mind, something might be different. Dear friend, it requires an adjustment of the rest of your days! Then you might fully ingest the reality that God raised his Son from the dead...that the end of the path is life...that the road to eternity is love. And that this reality is not the end, but the beginning.

It takes the cataclysm of an earthquake to announce the shattering of the old reality. It takes an angelic host, glistening in white, to chase the women's darkness. It takes soldiers, trembling and traumatized, to announce the reign of divine peace. It takes an empty grave to proclaim the eternal fullness of life. All of it orchestrated by the loving God that pushes the stars and planets on their way. It takes all of that to begin to melt the darkness through which these women grope in life, and it takes all of that to make us wake out of our slumber and encounter the foundation for living.

But what really transformed these women that glorious Easter morning wasn't all the commotion, but rather something deeper that touched their hearts—something that touches your heart, too. The one whom they loved met them face to face. "Hail," he said. That same friendly voice, always beckoning to his friends in support and encouragement. "Hail," he said. That same familiar voice, always assuring them to trust him—to trust God, inviting them and you and me to give him our lives, never to fear, never to ache. "Hail," he said, calling to them across what once was the great abyss of suffering and death, standing now before them, ready to resume the eternity of life, beckoning them to drop everything—everything they had ever thought to be true—and to follow him.

"Hail," he says. Do you hear him? He is risen, he is alive, and he is with you now! My friend, have you come, like the two Marys, groping through the dark to reverence his grave? You have two alternatives. Either you believe in his resurrection, and hence you believe in Jesus of Nazareth and the Gospel he preached, or you believe in non-resurrection and the fate of the grave AND you do not believe in Jesus of Nazareth and the Gospel he preached.   If Easter is not history, if Easter is not a present reality, we must become cynics. In other words, either we believe in resurrection and a living Jesus who is with us now in faith, and we surrender our lives and what we have to him, or we do not. Either we dismiss this good news as too good to be true, the fantasies of fickle women, or we permit ourselves to be overwhelmed by its absolute joy, thereby becoming overwhelmingly joyful people, brimming with laughter, courage and compassion.

Listen...did you hear that? "HAIL," a voice is saying. I heard it. Did you? He is risen. He is alive! And so are you and so am I, forevermore! Praise the Lord!

Chapter 17
A Glimpse of Easter Reality

*H*ow about a lesson in botany? You know, flowers and plants—green stuff. Have you ever heard of the Night-Blooming Cereus plant? Do you have one in your home? One of my parishioners did, and I actually saw it. The Night-Blooming Cereus blooms once a year. One night a year this glorious white bloom opens to reveal its magnificent beauty and fragrance to the world. By night's end, the flower closes and disappears. If you are not there on that fated night, with your eyes glued on the Night-Blooming Cereus, you miss the most glorious revelation of its awesome beauty. Then you must wait through the year, looking at this not terribly comely plant adorned with unsightly and threatening spikes.

It was the third day after the horror of Golgotha, a Sunday, which for the Jews was like our Monday, when everything returns back to normal. Life goes on, people go back to work, and not much has changed. Two men were slowly walking along the dusty road to Emmaus, and everything around those two people was returning so completely to normal that it was impossible to believe that either his life or his death was going to make any difference to the world at all. They began to fear that the whole business of his life had not really added up to much. Now he was dead, and somehow their future had died with him. They were, even now, moving beyond disappointment as they trudged along the road to Emmaus. But their heads still hung low, weighted by their dashed hopes. The ache in their hearts still showed on their faces, contorted with grief They were beginning to stoically accept that everything was as it had always been. You live and you die, and in the meantime you prepare for the worst.

Why were they going to Emmaus? Who knows? No reason is given—it was somewhere to go. But don't we all know why they were going to Emmaus? Emmaus is whatever we do or wherever we go to make ourselves forget that the world holds nothing sacred: that even the wisest and bravest and loveliest among us decay and die; that even the noblest ideas that men and women have ever had—ideas about love and freedom and justice—have always, in time, been twisted out of shape by selfish people for selfish ends. Emmaus is where we go, where those two went, to try to forget about Jesus and the great failure of his life. It's where we all go to hide from our disappointments (and I know that you can name at least one in your heart). Emmaus is where you go and check in, take a room for the night or a succession of days, at the Inn of the Chronically Disappointed, just off the road to Emmaus. You go there simply to withdraw, to be alone and sort something out. You go there to lick your wounds.

You know what it is like to walk down that road to Emmaus. It's a lonely road, isn't it? Even when you travel the road in the companionship of another. It is the road of broken dreams and dashed hopes, which no slick ads or glitzy TV commercials can wash away. Life has that almost infallible way of never turning out quite the way you hope or dream or plan, so you seek a haven...a resting place...an asylum, where you attempt to put it all back together, before you try again.

But sometimes, something strange can happen as you walk down that road to Emmaus. In those ordinary and unheralded backwaters of your life, a stranger appears—maybe not even a stranger, but just an awareness of a presence that you cannot explain. You just know someone or something is there. This presence appears at the most ordinary of times, in the least expected places or situations in your life.

What is most extraordinary about the Easter season is how ordinary are the appearances of Jesus. He is mistaken as a gardener, as a stranger on the road, as some unknown soul cooking breakfast on the beach. He comes to people in their grief, in their dismay, in their loneliness, in their confusion. You and I, had we written this resurrection scenario, would have done it differently. We would have given it the Cecil B. DeMille effect with strobe lights and brass bands and thousands cheering. But that wasn't the way it was, nor will it ever be—Jesus never approached from on high or from a superior position, but always in the midst of people, in the midst of real life and the questions that real life asks.

So it was on that dusty road to Emmaus. Consider something else with me about those two folks trudging down that road. Despite the burden of their grief and the aching of their hearts, they were still able to be hospitable. They invited a stranger to dine with them—to commune with them. Somehow they were still open to another person, and he a stranger. May that remind you how important it is to be open to a stranger—to welcome the stranger, if not strangeness, into your life.

And he sat down with them at the table and took some bread in his hands. As he broke it, suddenly they saw him for just a fleeting glimpse, just like the glorious, beautiful bloom of the Night-Blooming Cereus. One peek. One quick glimpse of awesome beauty in that smiling face of love that no hatred,

40

no power, can ever nail down, because love always prevails and overcomes. He was alive, blooming in the darkness. And just that one quick glimpse of beauty was enough—it is always enough—to suffuse life with peace and quiet joy and make every trek down to Emmaus bearable. You may now trust that you are never, ever, alone on the road. There is a presence walking with you. He is waiting calmly at the inn with bread to feed you. And the sacred moments, the moments of miracle, are indeed the ordinary moments. They are the moments when, if you look with your heart and listen with all your being and imagination, you become open to a real presence.

I am a man who has often been called a pessimist about life. I'm not, really. Actually, I am an optimist. I believe that if you hang in there and stare at the Night-Blooming Cereus all year, one night you will catch a glimpse of awesome beauty. And I think the Christian faith is often something like that. So often the Christian faith has promised far more than it can deliver, but perhaps you will catch a glimpse of the living Christ, in the unexpected place, if you open your heart and listen with all your being and imagination.

Yesterday, I learned that a most dear friend was told by his doctor that malignant cancer cells were found in the fluid in his lungs. I called him last night at the hospital, deeply saddened. But I felt a presence! Cereus had just bloomed in the darkness of the news.

Come, let us break bread together—a stranger is beckoning to us!

Chapter 18
The Resurrection—Simply Unbelievable

*W*hat moment in eternity was it, the moment when God could bear the pain no more? Was it in the deep darkness of Good Friday Evening? Or that kind of lifeless limbo of the Saturday Sabbath? Or amidst the fresh streaking rays of sunlight, dawning upon another sleepy Jerusalem morning? When was it, that the powerful yearning of God the Father for his absent Son Jesus reached such cosmic intensity that his love stretched down into the dank earth to embrace his child in his arms and lift him up to life?

The scriptures do not answer that profound question. Rather, they tell us a little story, remarkable in its simplicity, about women trudging in their grief to embalm a corpse, because that was the decent thing to do for one whom you loved. Women who, by tradition, could not testify in court because they were regarded as unreliable witnesses to the truth. Women standing before an empty tomb, terrified by its emptiness and its two angelic hosts. And old men, fickle in their loyalties to a friend and too numb and cynical to believe the women's words of wonder, running to see for themselves the linens neatly wrapped that had bound the body of God's Son.

First there is the women's fear, then the men's utter unbelief, and finally Peter's silent awe, mingling in the freshened air that morning. It is yet too early for alleluias—or fragrant lilies. There is simply stunned silence, because so great is the magnitude of what happened, that only this simple story can begin to capture reality as it begins to seep into creation.

The man mortally wounded on the cross—is alive! A dead man is alive again. Love walks the earth again. The huge tide of earth's history has been turned upside down. All its pain, all its suffering, all its sin, all its death are swept away when the Father reaches down into the ground to lift up his fallen Son. And the Father's heart, brimming with love, spills out to embrace all that he has made, including you and me, because his Son is one of us. All your pain and all your suffering and all your sin and all your death and dying is swept up in his mercy and engulfed this day by your Father's love. And as certainly as he has risen, so shall you rise. So shall you rise beyond life's darkest moment!

No wonder there was first fear, then unbelief, and finally silent awe in the early hours of that first Easter morn. This is too much to get the head around.

There were, and still are, no categories of human experience into which you can fit this event, like the final piece dropped into a complex puzzle. This is reality without precedent, astonishing. Only a simple story can reach into your heart and whisper the words that have excited life again: He is risen!

Find a silent moment, my Easter friend, a silent moment to go there yourself. Step across the threshold, your limbs trembling and your heart pounding, into the emptiness of his tomb where the linens are neatly stacked. Let his love embrace you and let this new day seep into your bones. Or spend a moment this afternoon with the stranger at the Inn of Emmaus, and let your heart be warmed and your eyes opened in recognition when the bread at the table is broken. Or huddle a moment this evening with those close to you in the shelter of a safe room, and let the living Christ show you his wounds, that he may share your woundedness.

The true joy of Easter dawns slowly, my friend, because it is so difficult to surrender your old ways of thinking about yourself, your life, and your world and to enter into this breathless new eternity God has given you. Like Mary Magdalene, you would prefer to cling to what is familiar, just as she turned to the gardener at the tomb and hugged her old teacher. But the Risen Jesus lifts up his little lamb and, pushes her in a profoundly new direction, telling her to tell others the astonishing, breathtaking new reality she experienced that morning at life's tomb: "I have seen the Lord!"

The great Russian novelist, Leo Tolstoy, once commented on how Russian peasants used to greet one another joyously with the acclamation, "Christ is risen!" They greeted one another as though this astonishing moment had just happened to them. And so I greet you, my friend, like a Russian peasant: Christ is risen!

Chapter 19
Why Are We Weeping?

She stands there at the tomb, sobbing, weeping, shaking in grief, like anyone who goes to hallow the grave of a beloved. She weeps, and her tears moisten the holy ground. The dawn of a new day is still concealed by the tears that cloud her heart as well as her eyes. The emptiness of the tomb is no comfort or consolation to one who has yet to realize that she is the first witness to the ultimate grace and grandeur of the living God. Morning has broken for Mary Magdalene. And mourning has broken her heart.

You must hear beyond the alleluias of an Easter morning to perceive the stunning tenderness and mystery of this story. This woman cannot begin to comprehend what has happened. It does not fit in her world. And, in humbleness, you also ought to admit that the message, "He is risen," is beyond your comprehension.

A voice calls out to her, "Woman, why are you weeping?" It is the gentle voice that will call out across the ages to all whose hopes of love and grace have been dashed. "Why, my beloved, do you weep?" She cannot yet recognize the risen Christ, standing before her, transforming the old world, as the new world breaks in from his streaming beauty. Easter dawns slowly, often in solitude, upon those who grasp the magnitude of its meaning. It takes time for us to let go of our world and enter the lofty levels of the new world that has dawned this day.

She mistakes him for the gardener! Couldn't God have chosen a more perceptive, a more reliable, person to inaugurate Easter than a woman whom no one would believe? Why does Easter begin with Jesus's appearance to Mary, rather than to one of those regular disciples? Why is this woman the first to behold the Lord of Life?

Do you remember who Mary is? She is the one follower whom Jesus personally healed! She is the one follower to whom Jesus personally reached out, taking her hand and lifting her up from the brokenness of her life, restoring life and vitality to her broken spirit. It was to a wounded one that this wounded healer reveals what every human heart yearns for: the Good News that death has been overcome, and that life blossoms amidst the desert. That love has triumphed! *The risen Christ draws closest to those who need him most.*

As she turns toward him a second time, he says, "Mary!" And her sudden moment of recognition occurs when he speaks her name. The Great Shepherd knows each of his sheep by name and touches their hearts with his gentle words of hope.

Hear the voice of the Risen Christ. He is speaking to you. He is calling you by your own name. He is reaching into your woundedness, whatever it may be, with his healing ways. He is raising you to your feet to stand with him, big as life can be, and he is gathering you together, in fellowship, with all those for whom he poured out his life.

And Mary, the wounded one, rushes down the road from the tomb into this thrilling new life with words that will forever turn the world upside down: I have seen the Lord!

In 1982, another woman went to a tomb. The *Washington Post* quoted then Vice President George H. W. Bush after he returned from a visit to the Soviet Union: "An amazing thing happened at the funeral of Soviet leader Leonid Brezhnev. Things were run with military precision; a coldness and hollowness pervaded the ceremony—marching soldiers, steel helmets, Marxist rhetoric, but no prayers, no comforting hymns, no mention of God. I happened to be in just the right spot to see Mrs. Brezhnev. She walked up, took one last look at her husband, and there, in the cold gray center of that totalitarian state, she traced the sign of the cross over her husband's chest. I was stunned."

Today is the day of God's sweetness and joy. Today is the day of life's hope and promise. Today is the day when we stand tall before the world and dare to live life with self-abandon. Now nothing can overcome the hope in Christ, neither cross nor tomb nor totalitarian state. Go in peace this day under the sign of the sacred cross of the Risen Jesus and share the stunning vision of Mary: I have seen the Lord!

Chapter 20
Console and Encourage My People

There was a Levite, a native of Cyprus, Joseph to whom the apostles gave the name of Barnabas, which means "Son of Encouragement." He sold a field that belonged to him, then brought the money, and laid it at the apostles' feet.
Acts 4:36, 37

I am going to ask you a very personal question. I alert you, because it is not the kind of question you are very often asked. You might want to reflect upon this question before your heart thrusts out an answer. Here is the question: do you like your name? No, I am not talking about the name you may have acquired through marriage. I mean, do you like your first name, the name that your parents gave you, long before you had a choice to say who you are? Do you like your first name? You know, of course, that it is a precious possession. It was given to you long before you could remember. You could only receive it.

You live with it. Few people ever change it. It was given to you, so now you seek to make something of that name. Oh—you say you don't much like the name given to you? If you don't, how would you change it? Would that change *you*? Somehow, our names begin to suggest our identity. Change the name, and you change the identity of a person. Or change the name, and you tell us something about the person and a new found identity. What would happen to you, if someone changed your name? Could you accept it? Will you consider, with me, that it might change you profoundly?

Names are very personal and precious things. To change them means to change the world. Sometimes, in the Bible, you hear about someone whose name was changed. Let us consider such a person who became a follower of Christ. He became a Christian, and so profound was the change in that person, that his name was changed. Like Simon, son of Jonah, who became Peter, or like Saul, who became Paul, consider Joseph whose name was changed to Barnabas, which means, "Son of Encouragement...Son of Consolation."

Perhaps you have wondered what it really means to be a follower of Christ. Let me tell you that it may mean (if you are ready to hear this) to have

46

that which is most precious to you—your personal identity—changed. So deep is the transformation in this enterprise we call the Christian faith, that what we take to be our most personal possession—our names—can be changed.

So they used to call him Joseph...but now they called him Barnabas, Son of Encouragement, Son of Consolation. His life was profoundly changed, and so was the little church of Jesus Christ. The profound transformation of this man altered the course of this little church's history. Would so profound a change in you and me make such a difference?

Something happened to Barnabas which no one in the New Testament seems to recall. Something seized this man. Who knows what he struggled with at night as he lay on his pillow, reviewing his life? But something happened. Nothing could compare with the power he had encountered. Nothing was as sweet as the love that now consoled and encouraged him. He was rich in a way he had never been before in his life. So he rushed out and sold a piece of property. (God and God alone knows what drove him to do this. I guess he didn't need those kinds of things anymore.) He sold a piece of property and he said, "Take it...use it...I have seen something that excels anything I have ever seen before. Use it to the grace of God, so that others might know the comfort of God's consolation and God's encouragement."

That image of Barnabas haunts and challenges Christian folk today. Does it inspire you with the same generosity? The real estate transaction of Barnabas is nothing more than Gospel-centered ministry. What does this mean to you, here and now, as you try to make sense of what is happening in your life in your little corner of the earth? Is there a spirit stirring deeply beneath the surface of your life? Is the power of the eternal Christ, more beautiful than anything you have ever known, urging you to respond like Joseph...now named Barnabas?

They called him the Son of Consolation, the Son of Encouragement. Apparently there were times in the life of the earliest church when zeal flagged and optimism waned. God knows that there are such times in your life when you need to have someone speak words of comfort, words of hope. Words from someone who has the vision to see beyond the narrow horizon that presses and limits your life. Joseph, now Barnabas, served that particular vital task amongst his brothers and sisters. When they gathered—down and out, confused and tired, bereft of any spirit—Barnabas reminded them what he had seen. He told them of the Christ who had touched him and changed his identity. Gazing beyond the horizon, he lifted their spirits with an imperishable hope for the future of each one of them.

You know, I think we need some small groups, some Circles of Barnabas, in the churches where the sons and daughters of consolation and encouragement can minister to one another through Christ. What do you think? It could be risky—names might be changed—but we might also be seized by that same power and confidence for life which sent Barnabas out one morning to sell his field and profoundly transform his world with God's Word of comfort, consolation and encouragement.

Chapter 21
The Craziness of Grace

*I*f you tell someone today that you have had an out-of-body experience, you may be assured that you'll get an invitation to tell your story on a TV news magazine. Is there anyone who isn't intrigued by the stories people tell of hovering over operating tables as their hearts stop in surgery, or returning to life from a fatal episode saying that they were bathed in a warm light and unspeakable peace?

They call these out-of-body experiences, and they suggest rumors from the threshold of eternity. I have never heard of anyone saying of someone else, "Look! That person—the one over there—is having an out-of-body experience!" It's always very personal and private.

But there were some people who thought that Jesus was having an out-of-body experience—or at least that his mind had become detached from his body, and something else was running him. In other words (dare we say it?), they thought he was mad...crazy...a lunatic! He must be beside himself...out of his mind.

His career would be launched a few spectacular miracles later. He comes home for a bite to eat, a family dinner, and suddenly a crowd is milling around outside, calling to him, knocking on the door, until the family couldn't even get a bite in edgewise. The little boy from Nazareth was a fantastic success, and if this continued he would end up with a chair in his honor at the Capernaum Institute of Pastoral Care.

But others could see here only madness and craziness. Some religion scholars from Jerusalem (the scribes) came down to the hometown and said, "Yep, he's crazy. Out of his mind. Something has seized him. It's voodoo, black magic, witchcraft, New Age thinking. He's in league with the devil (something often said when we cannot grasp or believe what we see)." It was academic blindness—the scribes could not see with their hearts, only with their minds. They could not see what was before their eyes. Only the sick and broken and troubled recognized the grace of God before them. *Pain recognizes love.*

Even his family could not recognize him for who he was (which might remind you that those closest to you don't always know who you really are). The people who knew him best—those who had lived with him the longest—

out of sheer embarrassment, were the first people in his public ministry who tried to silence him. What went through the heads of his family when they saw what was happening? Fear for the family's name? Fear for his welfare? Fear about his fame? Or maybe they recalled that they had always thought he was a little, um, strange growing up.

Religious scholars from Jerusalem looked at Jesus with virtually the same response: he's crazy! And, my friend, the world still thinks he is, as well as his followers when they dare to follow him.

The world cannot get its head around grace when grace stands in the midst of it. Such grace is too big, too awesome, too wondrous, too incredible, too overwhelming. This grace sweeps aside our carefully constructed notions of what is just and what is fair.

They didn't know who he was—they didn't recognize him—the scholars and the intellectuals. Neither did those who knew him best over the years, because you only know grace from the heart. You only know grace when a love beyond belief seizes your heart. The inner storms go silent, and you are bathed in peace. Only those who were hurting could recognize in Jesus the source: the divine madness of his Father's love. And, dear friend, this is called grace, and it is a gift. Grace is the acceptance of all that is unacceptable. Those who hurt have nowhere else to turn. They will risk the craziness of Jesus to be whole.

And how about you? Perhaps you are familiar with this man. You've known him all your life. His name is often on your lips, you are part of his family. Or perhaps he is someone new to you. Someone you have been seeking, without even knowing it. Are you ready to share in his madness, rather than falling back upon your feeble and failing efforts to get it right? Are you willing to surrender to this divine craziness called grace, which seems like the essence of the world's weakness, in order to hear your Father say, "You are my beloved, and your name is written in heaven!"

Are you willing to live in this passion of God for you? Do you, immersed in his crazy love, dare to risk the regard and esteem of others?

If so, I can promise you an out-of-mind kind of experience. You will know the madness of God—and you will be made whole.

Chapter 22
Have No Fear Little Flock

*F*or several years I made a number of transatlantic flights aboard an airline about which I had some doubts. Flying east across the vast expanse of the Atlantic Ocean was no problem—the flights were smooth and my blood pressure normal. Flying back, however, into the turbulent winds was another matter. Just enough bounce to make me ask, "What am I doing in this bucket of bolts, suspended eight miles above a vast cauldron of churning water that is fathoms deep, hundreds and hundreds of miles from the remotest possibility of land, buoyed up by a few jet engines (and we all know from our lawn mowers and automobiles what cantankerous things engines can be), distracted from reality by flight attendants with drinks and snacks and (Yes!) even meals. What am I doing in this airplane?"

I know how safe flying is supposed to be—and indeed it is—but that isn't quite convincing or consoling at that moment. So I shut my eyes, yearning for that welcome shudder of the landing gear extending itself. Don't tell me that people are incapable of profound faith. It requires profound faith to fly, at least for me

They weren't flying. They were sailing into the night across the Sea of Galilee, a huge freshwater lake more than 700 feet below sea level and surrounded by hills and cliffs. A sudden northerly draft would turn the glassy Galilean sea into a churning, seething caldron of death.

Suddenly, out of nowhere, a storm is raging (out of nowhere is how most storms in life come upon us), a boat is sinking, and twelve disciples, some of whom were seasoned sailors and fishermen on this very sea, are panicking for their lives. They surge to the stern where Jesus sleeps peacefully on a little pillow, awakening him with their terrified shouts, "Rabbi, don't you care that we are dying?" How could he care at that moment? He was sound asleep, cradled in the arms of his Father's love.

Awakened, he brushes the sleep from his eyes, and then he muzzles—gags—the wind. Yes, that's the word! *Muzzle* or *gag*—the same word Mark uses when Jesus earlier cleansed a raging demoniac. Now, having harnessed this wild force, Jesus says to the sea, "Peace—be still!" The wind ceased, and there was a dead calm. Moonlight reflected off the glassy sea, and not a ripple could be heard lapping at the boat. Just calm. S-E-R-E-N-I-T-Y!

He didn't turn on the weather channel to check the Doppler radar or to see if gale force winds were forecast. Rather than a meteorological diagnosis, he made a theological diagnosis and calmed the spirits of life's storms with an authority that left the disciples gaping in awe and wonder.

"Why are you afraid?" he asked, "Have you still no faith?" What is he talking about, "...still having no faith?" Did he expect them to stand there on the deck and just take a beating from the storm or get washed overboard to drown in the sea? Is that the great notion of "having faith?" That sounds more like the foolish denial we all engage in when we fly across the Atlantic in a jet.

Or does his question, "Have you still no faith?" mean, "Do you really know who you have on board with you? Do you know who is here to ride out this storm with you?"

No, they didn't know, really. They didn't yet know that this enigmatic sailor would soon trim his sails and boldly sail into the darkest storm. No, they didn't know yet that his little ship would run aground on Golgotha and his beautiful life would seemingly end, nailed to two crossed planks. No, they didn't know yet that, even in this worst of storms, when life's clouds are darkest, his Father was still holding him in his arms, just like that stormy night he dozed on the pillow. No, they didn't really know who was on board with them.

But we do. The whole story of Jesus in the Gospel of Mark is told so that we may know who is on board with us in stormy times. He is the one who says, with ultimate authority, whether over humankind or nature: PEACE. BE STILL.

Have no fear, little flock. St. Paul, who withstood many a storm in his life, both literally and figuratively, could pen such powerful and comforting words: Who, then, shall separate us from the love of Christ? Shall hardship, or distress or persecution or famine or nakedness or peril or sword? No! For I am persuaded that neither death, nor life, nor life's storms, nor principalities or powers, nor anything else in all of creation will be able to separate us from the love of God in Christ Jesus. When Christ Jesus is on board your ship, when he is at the center of your life, why are you afraid?

Chapter 23
Snapshots of Grace and Love

Some people say that a picture is worth a thousand words. A picture may be fuller in meaning, more descriptive of detail, and reveal more to us than many spoken words. We who preach must use spoken words to communicate to and with our people. We must depend upon words that often seem to just float around in the air.

Our scriptures are spoken words that have been written down. The scriptures, although simple, humble words, often create pictures for us to behold. Consider the *Word* who became flesh and lived among us, the Word that offers us a picture of God's care and compassion for his people.

I would like to invite you to look at two pictures painted by the scriptures. The first picture is painted with the words of the Twenty-third Psalm. It is the beloved picture of the shepherd caring for his sheep. God is the shepherd and we are his sheep. The Lord is *your* shepherd—you shall not want or desire for anything. He leads you beside cool and refreshing waters—bids you to lie down in lush and green pastures. You feel safe lying down and resting there in this richness. You feel secure and free from harm because God is with you. He is close to you, sheltering you. This is a picture of safety, comfort, and the nearness of God.

The Gospels expand and enlarge this picture of the Good Shepherd. There, in the lush green pastures, the Good Shepherd calls you by your given name, for he knows the name of each and every one of his sheep. You are known to him personally, and you know his familiar voice and respond to his bidding. Your relationship with the Good Shepherd is deeply personal and profoundly intimate.

Yea, though you walk through the valley of the shadow of death, you will fear no evil. Because the Good Shepherd is with you. Each of us will one day walk through that valley of death, and for some it can be a lonely trek. But you are not alone. The Good Shepherd accompanies you. The one who entered death, so very alone in god-forsakenness, has walked through death into eternity. He now walks with you. In the loneliest moments, at the end of your life, you will not be alone! The Good Shepherd, the wounded shepherd, walks beside you.

Another picture—from the Gospel of Mark, the fifth chapter. A man encounters Jesus. He is a deeply troubled person. Mark says that he is possessed by an unclean spirit. He sounds like someone we would call today a mentally ill person—someone who should be on the psychiatric ward of the hospital. This man lives outside the city, crouching amid the tombs and graves of the dead. No one dares to come near him. The townspeople have tried to restrain him with chains and shackles, but he, in his frightening strength, smashes the chains. No one can subdue him, calm him, or comfort him. Night and day, amongst the tombs and graves of the dead, he shouts in hollow pain. He picks up rocks and hits himself, bloodying his body. He is a troubled man—a lonely person—a totally isolated soul.

Perhaps you have seen a picture of the east, outside wall encircling the city of Jerusalem. A road runs between the east wall of the bustling community of Jerusalem and the Mount of Olives. If you sit on the Mount of Olives and look across the road to the east wall of Jerusalem, you will notice white stones all along the wall—outside the city. They are gravestones. The cemeteries were always just outside the cities' walls. This man lived surrounded by the dead, totally isolated from human contact, a lonely and terrified soul. The community regarded him as the "living dead." The people, in their fear, shunned him.

When I lived in Africa, there was no medication available to treat people who were HIV-positive or suffering from full-blown AIDS. Their communities shunned them. Their villages sent them away. That is when I came to understand what it meant for a person to be seen as the living dead. Human beings, in their fear, can be unspeakably cruel.

But the Good Shepherd of Psalm 23 reaches out from the Old Testament psalm to this man in his agonizing loneliness. He meets the man and frees him from the prison of his isolation among the living dead. He walks with the man, entering into that fenced-in space of loneliness that no one else has been able to enter. He says to the man, "You are not alone!" He says to each one of us, fenced into our own private space of loneliness, "You are not alone. Fear no evil, for I am with you!" And the Good Shepherd leads this man from the place of the living dead into green pastures, beside calm and still waters, and spreads a banquet of love before him.

The man is healed. He leaps for joy. His emptiness is filled. His loneliness disappears in the face of love. He wants to follow Jesus, but Jesus sends the man home to his family and those who would now be his friends. The man clambers over the wall and out of the place of the living dead, back into the community of caring human relationships. He has been saved—a lost sheep sought out, in his loneliness, by the Good Shepherd. And forevermore, he will not be alone!

When you can trust just that—that you are never alone—then you, too, will know the wholeness and abundance of life. And that, my friend, is called salvation!

Chapter 24
Dreams As the Ultimate Faith

*W*hat we so deeply need today are truthful dreamers—we do not need cynicism, vulgarity, self-centeredness, despair, resignation or status quo seekers. We need people who dare to dream the truth and to risk living that dream.

Jesus was standing and teaching in the midst of a huge, pressing crowd of humanity. Suddenly he recognized the contorted face of a man pushing through the crowd to reach out to him. Jesus had seen that face not long before, staring at him in the synagogue during worship when Jesus had healed a man possessed. The man now straining to reach him was Jairus, a leader of the synagogue, a member of the church council. Jesus paused and stared. Why would such a man of high status wish to approach him?

This man of great distinction and honor throws himself at the feet of the wandering rabbi, and Jesus sees the tears dripping down his face. Now Jairus is begging, pleading in anguish, "My little daughter is at the point of death. Come and lay your hands on her, so that she may be made well and live." The Master of Love leaves the crowd and goes with him.

What can be more devastating than for a parent to sit next to the deathbed of a little child? A child's death means so much more than the death of us old folks. A child's death means the death of hope. It challenges the very goodness of God. It shakes the foundations, and the wound never really heals. Answers are scarce at such moments.

But what if Jairus had accepted reality? What if he had remained at his little daughter's death bed, remained practical, accepted reality, and chosen to live with the inevitable? The little girl would have died. She would have been forever lost from his life. And he, Jairus, would have died too, a hollow, aching soul.

So what is happening here, as he throws himself at the feet of his last hope, the last shred of love in which to trust? Jairus moves from "having a faith" to "living a faith." He shifts from what may be called a comfortable belief system into a radical openness and a trust deeper than he had ever known or ever lived. From living his life as a cautious, culture-pleasing, church-pleasing leader, Jairus becomes a radical risk taker...a dreamer...a person of hope! Stripped of religion, he becomes a person of faith—a dreamer—because he has seen the love that invites us to dream.

The world is not comfortable with dreamers. Reality must be tamed, carved down to fit in a box. People come from his house to tell him that his daughter has died. "Accept reality," they counsel him. "Don't bother the teacher." They might as well have been telling him, "Go on home and die with her!"

Thank God for the ultimate dreamer, Jesus, who says to this distraught father, "Come on! Let's go!" When they arrive at Jairus's home, they find that the little girl's mother has already accepted reality. She has arranged for the professional mourners to begin their wailing, announcing the period of mourning. The crowds who have gathered at Jairus's home laugh—yes, laugh—at Jesus's strange diagnosis that real death has not yet occurred. Crowds and groups can often tend to foster cynicism or unbelief. Crowds are not bent upon the vagaries of dreamers.

Then, in one of the most touching and powerful moments in the Gospels, Jesus takes Jairus and his wife and three associates into the privacy of the little girl's bedside. Taking the little girl's hand, God's ultimate dreamer speaks the creative word, lifts the little girl to life, and hands her to Jairus and her mother. This father, overwhelmed with joy, embraces his precious daughter.

But what if Jairus had not been a dreamer? Would the little girl's mother have seen the miraculous happen? We need dreamers like Jairus to challenge and reveal to us realists that there is infinitely more possibility in this world when we trust in a reality that is bathed in divine love.

And what, again, would have happened to Jairus, had he not thrown all conventionality to the breeze? What if he had assented to all the counsel about realism, all the constraints of an ordinary religious life? What would have happened had he not risked it all?

And you wonder what your own life would resemble if you were to pursue Jesus with the same intensity and readiness and sense of immediacy as Jairus carried with him to the feet of Jesus. What would the spiritual landscape of the whole Christian world resemble?

And you also wonder what Jairus was feeling when he got up to get his revived daughter a peanut butter and jelly sandwich, his hands quivering with joy and his tears soaking the loaf of bread with ecstasy. Jairus must have known such tremendous mystery and awe at the God who walked this earth.

And what would happen if you risked dreaming your loving Father's dream for you?

Chapter 25
Losing and Finding Life

*T*hey were waiting for his final words of encouragement before they tested their wings. This was their first real try at being "disciples." But they didn't yet know themselves as disciples. They were simply some ordinary fellows—dreamers and discontents—hoping that there was something more to life than catching fish and collecting taxes and going to school and getting up at six o'clock in the morning, day after dreary day.

Like anyone else who has ever entrusted himself or herself to a leader, they knew they could bail out if the going got too rough. They could always go back to their family, and surely the family would take them in. There was some security in that. And few leaders ask for someone's life, unless in times of war. Jesus was so gentle, he wouldn't do that. So there was some security in that.

Yes, these first impatient followers of Jesus of Nazareth, excited about their first foray into the word as disciples, waited eagerly for him to get through his lecture and give them his final rousing words of encouragement.

It had not occurred to them that he might ask for their souls! Or suggest that true life is lived, ultimately, in vulnerability.

But ask for their souls, he did. He closed his commissioning with these anything-but-gentle words which exploded within their hearing, "I have not come to bring peace, but a sword!" Your family relationships will be threatened by turmoil. Shoulder crosses shall press upon you. Life lost for my sake will mean entering life for the first time. Boy, that was some send-off. Don't you think they kind of flinched when he patted them on the back and whispered these words in their ears?

And don't you kind of flinch or squirm when you hear Jesus triggering these spiritual grenades? I know I do, because he touches what I struggle most to create: a bit of security and peace of mind. I find it very hard to welcome into my life anything so disruptive of family, or as threatening as relinquishing control of my life, especially considering how hard I have worked to secure it. I am quite comfortable God walking next to me, but don't invade my family and especially not my private zone of personal security. Soothe me, Lord, but don't stir me up.

There is one word of consolation for us. It took those twelve dreamers and discontents the better part of their lives to figure out for themselves—for *themselves*—what he meant when he said, "Those who lose their life, for my sake, will find it." Not until they beheld with their own eyes the vulnerability of their master, not until they felt in their hearts the risks of true compassion for other human beings, not until they risked becoming weak and vulnerable, did the truth of Jesus's explosive words begin to fill their bodies with a new strength, their hearts with a new courage, and their minds with a vital hope.

The Master of the Twelve Dreamers and Discontents, our Risen Lord, continues to stir rather than soothe. He continues to challenge as a way of comforting. He continues to whisper in our ears the words of freedom: those who lose their life, for my sake, will find it.

I think of the couple who rip up deep roots in the community to nourish the souls of a tiny band of Christians in a faraway country. I think of the young man who abandons destructive friends and peers to find himself and his wholeness. I think of the young mother with an armful of children, studying the faith, and opening a shelter for the homeless. I think of the person, life draining from the body, thanking God for all the people who have cared and shared the few precious moments of life that remain.

These are not great saints about whom books will be written. No, they are just some of the many who have heard the Master's words, "Those who lose their life, for my sake, will find it." We are all dreamers and discontents, not always aware that our yearning for "something more" means yielding to "something less." It is the mysterious way of the divine—to yield, to surrender, to risk everything, even what God loves most. For this is finding life, living life, drinking from the fountain of eternity.

So hearken to the whisper, listen to the sigh deep in your heart. It is the spirit of God conversing with one whom he loves: If you lose your life, for my sake, you will find it!

Chapter 26
Plant a Radish, Get a Weed?

*I*have been troubled by an experience I had a few years ago. I had a most enjoyable opportunity to preach at the 100th anniversary of the church in Connecticut where I began my ordained ministry. After the service, later that afternoon, I remarked to a colleague that the Order for Confession had been omitted from the service. I wondered why. I knew that it was permissible to do so on major festivals, but that day was a minor festival. My colleague replied that a commentary on the *Lutheran Book of Worship* suggests that confession is not essential to worship and may be omitted, which was now the practice at this parish as well as the one he had supply-preached at that very morning. I was disturbed.

When I had finished preaching the sermon, I sat down next to an elderly pastor from a conservative Lutheran tradition who ministered part-time at this parish. He purred to me, in a quiet deep voice, "It is unusual and refreshing to hear a young man (young man!) preaching like that today."

Suddenly I found myself located in a conservative religious position, connected to another passing generation. All because I had implied that there was something like evil in the world—in each one of us—and that managing this reality, as well as sin and destructive guilt, just might be something that the God of infinite love and compassion had entrusted to his church as its fundamental work.

My good friend Brennan Manning once said to me, "You know, Lou, I travel throughout the country, preaching and leading retreats. What utterly overwhelms me is the amount of self-hatred I see in people. It is tragic."

Indeed, it is. And it is even more tragic that the church should blind itself to these realities by omitting its confessions. It is tragic, for only the words of the gracious, loving Father, who can accept the evil in us, can liberate the human soul from self-hatred—from the power of what is truly evil.

Consider with me one of Jesus's most intriguing and powerful parables. Someone owned a field and sowed good seed in it. He trusted the earth to yield the fruits of its goodness. He trusted that life was orderly, like the chorus in the Broadway musical, *The Fantastics*: "Plant a radish, get a radish!" But life is seldom so clean. In the night, while everyone is sleeping, an enemy sows weeds in the field. Outside of their awareness, when they are most vulnerable, when they can do nothing about it, the field is contaminated. And the master says, "We are going to have to live with it." The servants implore the master—they want an answer, "Where did this evil come from?" The master simply says, "An enemy!" The identity of the enemy is irrelevant; its reality is fundamental. The story is not about from where evil seeds come from, or why evil things happen to people. Rather, that evil is there. It is real. It is part of us—of you and me and everybody else we know.

Henri Nouwen, in his book *The Road to Daybreak*, tells the story of a little four-year-old girl who found a dead sparrow in front of the living room window. The sparrow had flown into the window pane, killing itself. Little Jessie asked her father, "Where is the bird now?" To which he replied, "I don't know." "Why did it die?" she asked. "Because all birds return to the earth," he replied. "Then we must bury it!" said little Jessie. They processed outside with a napkin to use as a shroud, placed the sparrow in a box and, under a hand-made cross, buried the sparrow. Jessie's father asked, "Do you want to say a prayer?" Jessie folded her hands and prayed, "Dear God now we have buried this sparrow. Now you be good to her—or I will kill you, Amen". Her father said to her, "You didn't have to threaten God!" And she replied, "I just wanted to be sure." Weeds of evil sown amongst the wheat of innocent childhood.

And so what are we going to do about it? The servants ask the master, "Shall we go on a moral crusade, tear up all those weeds, clear the field to perfection?"

Do you, deep in your heart, in those hidden moments that no one else knows about, try to clear your own field? Do you work hard, pulling up all the weeds deep inside yourself, to make your life shine like an amber field of grain? The darnel sown in this field of Jesus's parable is virtually indistinguishable from the wheat. It is poisonous, and its roots entwine themselves about those of the wheat seedlings. My dear friend, there is no way you can march into the field of your life and tear out all your weeds without destroying yourself. And, furthermore, you don't need to! The master, infinitely patient and infinitely wise, accepts the contamination of his field and says, "Let them grow together, until the full fruits appear. Then there will be a harvest." Then there will be a harvest!

Consider all the judgments with which you have burdened yourself. All the judgments upon others. All the judgments about how you have lived your life and how it will turn out. All these judgments are suspended in the infinite patience and love of the master. There will be a harvest, in spite of the fields of contamination, and golden fruits will glisten.

God, rather than risk tearing up the roots of evil in us and destroying us in the process, becomes vulnerable, in his Son. He lets the evil have at Him, in order to allow his suffering love to overwhelm and obliterate all of our weeds. The cross—his Son's sacred cross—is the ultimate symbol that the evil, the sin, and the brokenness sown in all of us is forgiven. Not by your own power are your fields weeded, but by accepting the profound love of Him who gathers and delights in what will become ripe and mature fruit.

Not by the violence of a weed-eater can your fields be cleansed, but only by the patient, enduring, and determined love of a cross. Confession is the first step in the cleansing of your fields, in the cleansing of your life. First you must acknowledge the weeds sown outside your awareness. Then you must allow the master to weed your fields with His cross. After that come the fruits of true joy and true freedom.

Be silent, now, and dare to enter your heart. Look at the darkness, your deepest sin. See what troubles you most, the weeds in your garden sown by the enemy. Do not try to tear them up. The gardener with his cross removes them. Yield that burden to him which, as your servant, he is delighted to do. Now look at the wheat. That is in your field, shimmering and full of the fruit your Father has sown! Rejoice in the fruit that ripens rich within you.

Be patient with yourself. Be patient with others. Be full of the patience of the Master. A harvest is coming, and it is a harvest of wondrous joy and beauty. Be patient.

Chapter 27
I...My...Me...Mine

*P*erhaps you are old enough to remember mama's favorite remedy for childhood illnesses. Was it a stomach ache, a headache, a fever, constipation, or just plain old lethargy? Just give that kid a spoonful of cod liver oil and, wham! He or she was back on the road to health. And, believe me, that spoonful of cod liver oil worked. Do you know why? Because you had to get better, lest you face a second such spoonful the next morning. Marvelous medicine, but sometimes the remedy seems worse than the illness.

Something like that must have occurred to the young man who came to Jesus seeking, rather naïvely, a solution to what he thought was a legitimate problem. After all, he was only looking for a little bit of justice, a little bit of fairness, a little bit of help to get on with his life. But what he received from the Lord must have sent him reeling. If that has never happened to you, then you may not have ever bumped up against true religion!

A nameless person stepped out of a crowd and implored Jesus, "Teacher, use your influence to get my brother to divide the inheritance with me." It was a fair request, one that shows up often enough in the courts even today. Be fair—divide equally. What bothered this younger man was the fact that it was always the eldest child who received the inheritance of the land. Large plots of valuable crop lands and farms passed from generation to generation, always to the eldest child. That's the way it was in Palestine. And it does sound grossly unfair. Except that there was a reason why this happened.

To divide up, from generation to generation, the small amount of precious productive land into successively smaller and smaller tracts would deplete the productivity of the valuable crop lands. It would undermine the economy of a nation and destroy the very sustenance of a whole society of people. It was an invitation to famine and starvation.

Within this context, it becomes apparent how self-centered and inconsiderate this young man's request is. What is the center from which he lives his life? Obviously, the center is himself—he sees himself as an island in the sea of humanity. He has no moral qualms about risking the suffering of others in order to satisfy his personal appetites.

He came to Jesus simply asking for a little help with his problem, a little fairness...didn't he? But Jesus slices through this man's illusion and dishes up a spoonful of cod liver oil.

"Let me tell you a story," Jesus says. "The land of a rich man brought forth plentifully (When someone's land had brought forth plentifully and showered riches in Palestine, everyone thought the person had been blessed and favored by God.), and he thought to himself (his first mistake—he should have given gratitude to the source of the gift), 'What shall I do, for I have nowhere to store my crops?' And he said to himself, 'I will do this: I will pull down my barns, and build larger ones; and there I will store all my grain and my goods. And I will say to my soul (his innermost being), Soul you have it made!' But the voice of God whispered to him that night as he laid his head on his feathery pillow: 'You fool! This night your soul is required of you.' And he dies peacefully in his sleep. And his grain rots."

Did you notice in this little story that in the short space of three simple sentences, the word "I" is used six times and the word "my" five times in this man's frightening soliloquy? He is so wrapped up inside himself that he is oblivious to reality. He is a desert island, unconnected to any other life than his own. Disjoined from the divine goodness and source of life, the man is bereft of any human relationship except to himself; and his grain rots. When that young man who had approached Jesus heard this story, he could not have been anything other than pained by the mirror in which he saw himself.

This is strong medicine. We may not be as well as we thought we were. There is another way to live life. It offers a way to be centered in this world. Compare this young man seeking help, the rich man and all his grain, and the man Jesus. Compare the words of Jesus with the statements of these men. There are no more poignant words in scripture than when Jesus says of himself, "The foxes have holes and the birds have nests, but the Son of Man has no place to lay his head."

All that Jesus ever possessed was a profound and unwavering love for people—the likes of you and me—and he called it, "The abundant life!" He was connected with God and, therefore, profoundly connected with every human being. And that was enough.

How have you have heard these stories? They are strong medicine! Sometimes God's love is like that. I could suggest to you not to let your grain rot—it will. Perhaps your grain could feed someone. Only when you learn to share your grain do these harsher stories of Jesus have the power to heal, not like cod liver oil, but like the sweetest honey.

Chapter 28
His Hand Reaches Out for You

A tourist ventured too close to the edge of a canyon, lost his footing and plunged over the precipice, clawing and scratching to save himself. Somehow he was able to grab hold of a small, shrubby bush. Overwhelmed with terror, he cried out, "Is there anyone up there? Can anyone help me?"

Then he heard a reassuring voice say, "I'm here—the Lord your God."

The man replied, "I am so glad you came along. I can't hold on much longer."

The Lord replied, "Before I help you, I want to know if you believe in me."

"Lord, I certainly believe in you. I serve on my church's council. I chair a committee. I worship at least once a month. My pledge is reasonably current. You and I are on speaking terms for a pray when I need you. And, furthermore, my daughter attends a Lutheran Seminary."

"But do you believe in me?

The man was becoming desperate as clods of earth drifted down deep into the canyon. "Lord, you can't believe how much I believe in you. I believe!"

And the Lord said, "Good, now let go of the branch."

The man stammered, "But Lord..."

And the voice of the Lord came back, "If you believe in me, let go of the branch."

The man was silent for a moment. Then he yelled loudly, "Is there anyone *else* up there?"

A cute little story, but there ARE times in our lives when God says to us, "Let go of the branch."

It is the depth of night on the Sea of Galilee. Downdrafts from the steep cliffs whip up violent and sudden storms which turn the placid sea into a seething caldron. It is between 3 AM and dawn, a time when tired souls seldom trust their intuitions. The sea is frothing and waves are battering their tiny boat. There are no friendly lights glimmering from the shoreline, no stars to guide them. In exchange for doing what Jesus had told them, they now faced a watery grave.

But it wasn't the sea that terrified them—it was an apparition, as bright as St. Elmo's fire, coming toward them. If you had been there, even you would have thought it a ghost. Seized by fear, they wept in panic. Jesus, seeing their fear immediately spoke to them, "Take heart. I am coming to you. Do not be afraid."

But it is fear, always fear, that makes it difficult to see God. Fear that makes it difficult to trust God and to surrender to God. That is why it is so hard to let go of the branch. Peter responded, "Lord, if it is you—and I'm not so sure it is—command me to come to you on the water."

Jesus looked at him, their eyes fixed upon one another, and said one word: "Come!" Have you ever peered deeply into the eyes of Jesus? They beckon to you in one word: COME!

Peter stepped out of the boat and began striding across the tips of the waves until... Until he noticed how strong the wind was against his face. He began to teeter in the wind. Terror again seized his heart, as the water encompassed his waist and rushed toward his neck. Arms flailing, he cries out, "Lord, save me!"

Now, some point out that Peter got into trouble when he took his eyes off Jesus, and there is truth to that. But, personally, I don't know anybody who doesn't get distracted in life. I don't know anybody who hasn't sailed this same ship of doubt amidst the storms. I know no one whose trust alone would get him or her through the storm. I know no one who can live their lives better than Peter did it that night on the Sea of Galilee. None of us has that kind of faith. We will always avert our gaze. But that's not the point of this story.

Rather, what would have happened, in that critical moment of drowning, if *Jesus* had taken his eyes off *Peter*? Would Peter have disappeared beneath the seething waves? Matthew tells us, however, that Jesus, eyes fixed on his friend who took the risk, reached out his hand and caught him, clutched him to his breast in his wide embrace—Peter was safe!

Unlike Peter, Jesus does not become distracted. Jesus does not ask us to COME, to follow and surrender, without being within arms' reach to catch us when we inevitably flounder. Let go of the branch, because there is someone next to us. Someone is up there, waiting to grab us. Step out into the storm. Answer the voice that beckons, *"Come!* For there is a strange presence with us in the storm, a presence whose gentle hand reaches out to catch us. Wise is the one who travels through life with one hand outstretched, confident that someone will grasp that hand with power when the wind blows against us.

There is probably no more important task for a church than to be the place where people are taught to walk through life with one hand outstretched. You cannot hold this conviction, this perspective of faith, alone You cannot do it without the sacraments, without the story of the Savior, without a fellowship willing to share their stories about experiencing the hand that has reached out and saved them.

Perhaps no greater spiritual movement could be unleashed in the weakened Body of Christ today than if the fellowship broke its silence and shared its stories of faith with one another. Rest assured, Peter did. And so did the other eleven who, on a calm and tranquil night on the Sea of Galilee, knelt on that boat and worshipped Jesus. Can you not see them, hand in hand, with one another and with their Lord?

So my fellow sailor, if you can't let go of the branch, at least reach out to him and to one another, in whom he now lives.

Chapter 29
For Once, the Hard Truth

*I*magine yourself in the crowd as it weaves and lurches forward, as if straining to touch a priceless treasure. You aren't comfortable in crowds, but you are tagging along anyway, borne on the crest of waves propelling this sea of humanity forward. The crowd is moving in a certain direction—it is following someone. That someone is why you are part of this crowd—you are following him, too.

You want to get closer to him, maybe even touch him. Because he had said something that touched your world-weary soul. You heard words that had the ring of truth, for once. Not a slick political slogan, not a cute or sexy commercial, not an argument of bureaucratic doubletalk. For once, you heard words that were simple, truthful, compassionate, and understanding. He was hopeful. He promised life rather than death. And so you press with the crowd...toward him, your fragile soul, clasped tightly and protectively in your arms.

And then he turns and looks at *you*! His piercing eyes explore your waiting heart, and he speaks, "If you want to come to me and you do not hate your own father and mother and wife or husband and children and brothers and sisters and, yes, even your own life, you cannot be my disciple. If you do not bear your own cross and come after me, you cannot be my disciple. So, therefore, if you do not renounce all that you have, you cannot be my disciple."

And you are stunned, paralyzed as the crowd presses deafly along. Your world is shaken to the foundations. You are puzzled, baffled, hurt, confused. Because you heard him!

He made a mistake didn't he? He was misquoted, wasn't he? He didn't mean that, did he? *Hate. Renounce.* What kind of terrifying, all-consuming love lays such claims for loyalty upon the human soul?

When I prepared to write my sermon about this lesson, I asked a fellow pastor, "Upon which text are you preaching?"

"The second one," he answered.

To which I replied, "You are chickening out. Let me tell you, friend, once you read the Gospel lesson on Sunday morning, no one will hear anything else you have to say until you deal with these hard words of Jesus."

The lesson is softer in Matthew's Gospel, when Jesus says to you, there in the crowd, "Whoever loves father and mother more than me...is not worthy." At least he doesn't say "hate."

But you are still standing there in the crowd. What can I say to you about what he just said to you? I want to make it easier for you, somehow...and easier for myself! I could say to you that he didn't really mean what he said, and that Matthew is more accurate in softening it. But I have no authority for that. I could remind you that self-hatred and hatred in families is real, and that most murders in this society are the result of domestic violence. I could suggest that Jesus implies that a fundamental religious issue in life is entangled with family relationships and SELF. And I would feel somewhat more confident in suggesting that. In other words, our relationship to God requires us to deal with our relationships in family and to self. Or I could suggest that Jesus was deeply aware of a dark side in every human being—a hidden dimension—that fostered ambivalent feelings of hatred and love even toward those closest to us, and even toward our own selves.

But somehow all of this does not seem to get at what Jesus had in mind when he turned to the crowd and you heard him speak those shocking words. If anyone cherishes the notion that Christianity is for the weak-kneed and faint of heart, or that his followers are a bunch of nice old folks of like mind who smile their way through life, then that someone ought to have been standing there in that crowd. In fact, maybe the church ought to always position itself in the crowd to remind itself that we who call ourselves Christians are called to be cross-bearers. Not because bearing crosses is fun, but because there is no other way to follow this human embodiment of God's mysterious love.

But you are still standing there, frozen. Chilled by what he asks of you, if you want to draw near to him. Do you suppose that in these powerful words there just might be an unleashing of a grace, an unleashing of a love, that could liberate and transform you? Could it be possible that God just might create something new in you? What would happen if you were to surrender everything to him? Your whole heart, your whole soul, everything you have, everything you are, along with your self-hatred and hatred of others. Is it possible that every relationship you have would be transformed? That you would see every other human being, even yourself when God looks at you, with profound compassion and delight? Might such new vision give those other people their freedom to be themselves?

Go ahead now. Take that first step. Follow him. Touch him, as he has touched you. It's frightening. It takes incredible courage—some would call it foolishness. But it is God's foolishness. And he will give you back yourself, cleansed and brightened with the power to love others—your "loved ones"— as he has loved you.

Why are you standing there? He was speaking to you. He recognized you in that crowd, long before you saw him. He's waiting for you...to decide.

Chapter 30
The Redemption of a Crook

*C*ertainly, you have heard of people who speak of experiencing "turning points" in life—dramatic changes in the direction of their lives. Often it is painful upheaval which precipitates these dramatic changes, and anyone who has passed through one of these turning points is no longer the same person. Something else draws these persons, beckons to them. They have been changed, profoundly transformed, and their life and even their perception of reality will never be the same.

Have you ever experienced one of these turning points in your life? I'm not talking about one of those out-of-body experiences where you hover over the operating table and watch doctors trying to revive you. I doubt that anything quite that dramatic has happened to anyone reading this. Most of the time, I have seen people on the threshold of a turning points when they have come to me seeking help for a relationship that has gone awry, often with a spouse, with a child, with a parent, or with a friend. I could be a good therapist, if I wanted to, but I listen for something else. I am listening, listening deep, for the mystery of God. I am listening for a whisper of movement indicating that God is about to precipitate a turning point, one so profound and momentous that I have no other term to describe it than *a spiritual revolution.*

So perhaps my question really ought to be: have you ever experienced a spiritual revolution? Before you rush to answer, or to deny that such a thing has ever happened to you, let me tell you about someone who reached a turning point and survived a spiritual revolution.

His name was Jacob, well-known son of Isaac. A father of Israel. And a crook! Yes, a crook, a sociopath, a liar, a wheeler-dealer, a con man. That's one of the fascinating things about the Bible—it is so honest. Some of its heroes start out as absolute scoundrels. It reminds me that there is even a place somewhere for the likes of me...and you.

Evening is drawing nigh. The shadows are lengthening as Jacob peers across the Jabbok River, preparing himself to face his powerful brother, Esau. All his life he knew that someday he would have to face his brother again. Now terror seizes his heart—and with good reason.

Jacob had stolen what rightfully belonged to his brother—almost proving that honesty is not the best policy. He is remembering that night so long ago when he entered his father's tent. The old man was sitting there, blind and drooling like a child. What a pathetic sight. It didn't take much to steal the birthright from that old skeleton. You know, Jacob almost proves that if you are shrewd enough and try hard enough and bend a little bit, you can get what you want out of life. You want power? You can have it. You want wealth? You can have it. Of course, you have to lie a bit, be resourceful. Often the good things in life come to such folk.

I don't like this fellow Jacob. He abuses his parents And tonight, here at the Jabbok, he sends his wife and children across the river to edge toward his hostile brother. He uses his family as guinea pigs—or canaries in the mineshaft—to save his own hide. Not even his father-in-law trusted him. I don't like him—do you?

But I know there is something of him in me—in all of us—something that is quick-witted, sharp, willing to bend, frightened inside, nagged by our dishonesty with ourselves. It's so hard to be truthful! How can the Bible make room for people like him? Like you? Like me? Ah, but there is a turning point at hand.

Under the floodlights of the stars, in the deep chill of the night, Jacob falls asleep...only to awaken to a spiritual revolution. In silence, his troubled sleep begins. But this is more than a bad dream, as he thrashes on the ground, raising the dust from which he was created. It is more than a bad conscience that overpowers him in the depth of the night. It is a wild and fierce love, in the form (Amazingly!) of an angel, that he seeks to twist and control with all his strength and resources, as he had always sought to do throughout his life. Jacob is about to storm heaven with all his physical prowess, when a piercing pain radiates through his hip. Suddenly, he is wounded. Suddenly he is up against a power he can no longer control, or use, or turn to his advantage. Suddenly he is weakened, bereft of any strength. His ego bruised, reduced to a trembling whisper of surrender to this fierce and passionate love, he pleads: grant me a blessing.

In the morning he awakens, amidst the frost, a transformed person, limping across the Jabbok River into the waiting arms of his brother's love. Jacob will limp for the rest of his life. He will carry his wound with him, but he is no longer the same person. He has been touched by grace. He has experienced a spiritual revolution.

Perhaps you carry your wounds with you, in the silence of your heart. I often wonder what would happen to us, if we open ourselves to our woundedness. Would we be surprised? Surprised to discover that others, just like Jacob, limp alongside us, carrying the signs of *their* wounds? Would we be surprised to find ourselves in the company of another man, wounded in the hands and feet and side? A man somehow striding forth triumphantly, holding out his hand to us, as if he had just been raised from the dead by a love even wild enough to conquer that ultimate defeat?

This is a strange God, a wild, fierce, and compassionate God, that dwells in the Bible. This God caters not to our whims or even our needs. This God does not fit into the world of our ideas about how God should behave. But this God heals. This God transforms. This God blesses. This God graces the life of those who surrender, in emptiness, to be filled with his love.

If the story of Jacob means anything—if the story of Jesus means anything—the stories mean this: Open your wounds, no matter who you are, to the passionate love of God. If you can do that, you will experience a profound spiritual revolution: that peace which the world cannot give, that richness of love which the world cannot offer. A turning point, in life and death!

Chapter 31
Thou Shalt Not Peek

He also told this parable to some who trusted in themselves that they were righteous and regarded others with contempt: ¹⁰"Two men went up to the temple to pray, one a Pharisee and the other a tax collector. ¹¹The Pharisee, standing by himself, was praying thus, 'God, I thank you that I am not like other people: thieves, rogues, adulterers, or even like this tax collector. ¹²I fast twice a week; I give a tenth of all my income.' ¹³But the tax collector, standing far off, would not even look up to heaven, but was beating his breast and saying, 'God, be merciful to me, a sinner!' ¹⁴I tell you, this man went down to his home justified rather than the other; for all who exalt themselves will be humbled, but all who humble themselves will be exalted."

Luke 18:9-14

*H*is problem was that he had peeked. Yes, he had peeked—peeked while he was praying. Like a little child, looking around to see what others were doing, the Pharisee had peeked while he was praying.

Had he kept his eyes shut when he had gone up to the temple, he might not have ended up as one history's great characters of disdain. But take it easy on that peeker. He was a good man. Like you and me, he tried a little bit harder than most people. And we can applaud him for his effort, can't we?

Even if he was a peeker, please remember that he was a good man. If you take his self-assessment at face value, he becomes a role model of good behavior. He was faithful in his close relationships, honest and fair in his dealings with other people. No bribe would ever grease his palm—he was a man of impeccable character. And to top it all off, he was a good patriot, proud of and loyal to his nation. Not a traitor like that tax collector. He's a religious busybody, fasting twice a week when he had to fast only once a year. And, bless his heart, he tithed on everything he got—on his gross pay, when all he had to tithe on was his agricultural income. His only flaw seems to be...that he peeked while he was praying!

Now I know that in spite of my efforts to rehabilitate the character of this

Pharisee, there is something in him that you don't like. You want to point your finger at him and say that there is something despicable about him! Ah, but that is very dangerous, for to do so is to fall into the very same trap he has fallen into, which is to evaluate others. Luke reminds us that Jesus told this story for people who trusted themselves and despised others. So you *can't* despise him. Your heart has to go out to him. He is a tragic person. And herein lies the tragedy: It is axiomatic that:

1. You cannot accept others unless you can accept yourself.
2. You cannot love others unless you can love yourself.
3. You cannot be compassionate and forgive others unless you can be compassionate and forgive yourself.

This man is hurting deeply. This man is empty of self-respect, self-love, self-esteem. It is not that he despises others—in his own inner hidden world, he despises himself. And, as so often happens, it may have been his religion which taught him to despise and devalue himself.

Do you hear his prayer? Five times in his little prayer he mentions himself. His prayer is a monologue—a soliloquy—with himself at the center. He talks to himself! Just jabbers away. He is a very contemporary person whose spiritual dialogue has almost a desperate ring of yearning for love, yearning for grace in a vacuum, in an era when the reality of God has been eclipsed.

The poor man is frozen and frightened into a cube of life. He is terrified to open himself and let his brokenness, his pain, his sin rise to the surface...because he doesn't really believe. He hasn't ever known that there is a God who is a loving, caring Father waiting eagerly to say to him, "My child, I love you! My child, let me cleanse you. My child, I will make you perfect and heal your wounds and hold your trembling heart."

But, look! Off in the corner, another man is praying. He too hurts. His heart aches. He bears the burdens of a lifetime of failures and screw-ups, betrayals and illusions. He too despises himself, a man of little self-respect and self-esteem. He doesn't peek when he prays, because he knows there is nothing in this world that can fill the emptiness that cuts through to his heart. This is an emptiness that gnaws at his being each day at the toll booth and each night when he pulls the covers over his head. It is an emptiness that even chases him down the back alleys of his dreams in the depth of night.

He doesn't even consider himself worth talking to. He simply cries out, "God, be merciful to me, a sinner." And the story Jesus is telling abruptly stops. What happened next?

A priest I know once described his own experience. He says of himself, "One afternoon I dove under the covers, trying to hide myself. I felt unclean, like a moral leper scarred with sin. The same night I read a passage from the book by Nikos Kazantzakis, *Report to Greco*. An old man lies dying. He is filled with guilt and remorse because of his sinful life. At length he dies, and goes, naked and trembling, before the Lord. Waiting for judgment on his life. Jesus has a bowl of sweet-smelling ointment at his fingertips. He dips a finger into the sweet-smelling ointment and washes the man clean of his grime and shame. Then Jesus says, "Don't bother me with that stuff anymore. Go over and play."

My friend, the priest, concluded, "Suddenly, I was filled with peace. The compassion of Jesus enabled me to be compassionate toward myself."

Jesus says, "Don't bother me with that stuff...go over and play." Is such a statement too demeaning and playful, or is this very heart, the infinitely loving heart, of the message from the cross? Does it sound too cheap and too simple to be of God? Isn't this precisely what sent Jesus marching throughout Palestine to announce his Good News to all those whose heads hung low and whose hearts were heavy with sorrow? Isn't this the indescribable and infinite joy that ultimately radiates throughout the New Testament? Isn't this a playful clue to understanding that there is more joy in heaven over one sinner who repents than ninety-nine who have no need of repentance?

Two people went up to the temple to pray. One talked to himself. The other surrendered his broken heart and cried to God. So, my friend, when you pray, do not peek. Keep it simple, brief and to the point, and as honest as a person could ever be: "God be merciful to me a sinner." And you know what? As scandalous as it sounds, you just might hear a voice from heaven whisper: Don't bother me with that stuff—go over and play.

Chapter 32
The Stranger As a Holy One

*T*he man moved carefully through the sandy plains of Jesus's homeland, pausing along the way when he encountered an afflicted, troubled person. Almost haltingly, not with the greatest confidence, but more like a baby bird in its inaugural flight, awkwardly flapping its wings, the man stretched forth his hand, and gently laid it upon person's contorted and writhing body. Then he lifted his eyes heavenward and said, *"In the name of Jesus, be healed!"*

And, to his shock and wonder (the healer's, that is), the afflicted person was healed, made whole, and restored to life. The healer looked at his hands, overcome by the power that radiated from him when he spoke the name of Jesus, and he was filled with gratitude and praise for God's gift of life.

Meanwhile, a crowd of onlookers had been gathering. Several onlookers stepped out of the crowd, grabbed the man, forced him up against the wall with their powerful grip, and proceeded to threaten him for abusing the name and the power of Jesus. "Don't ever do that again," they threatened him. "You are not one of us...you do not belong to us...you have not been empowered to do this the way we have. You don't have the right credentials—you're not licensed to use the name of our teacher."

Later that day, the onlookers told Jesus what they had done to keep the movement pure. Maybe they were jealous, because this unauthorized healer, who was not one of them, was successful. Maybe they were frustrated, because they couldn't stop the unauthorized healings. The disciples proudly told Jesus all that they had done to stop this man.

For a long time, whenever I read or heard this story, I had the picture of this healer as a charlatan, or at least a shady character, operating outside the boundaries of the American Medical Association. A quack, so to speak, who saw a quick way to make a buck.

But let's try to think about this peculiar healer another way. What if he were genuine? Apparently, he had never met the Lord face-to-face, but what if he were someone who had seen Jesus, was profoundly moved, and then saw people suffering and said to himself, "I'll give it a try." In other words, what if there is a child-like innocence in this man who simply takes the gifts of God at face value and tries them out? And, when he sees it work, tries it again?

What do you think that man felt like, when he got shoved up against the wall by Jesus's own followers, threatened with a lawsuit, and told to cease and desist, or Peter would take him fishing at the bottom of the Dead Sea? The innocence of a child-like faith, violated by the disciples' notion of rectitude and order! Somehow Jesus's disciples had gotten the notion that they had position or privilege by virtue of their selection—that there were "ins" and "outs" in the Jesus Movement.

The stranger didn't seem to bother Jesus. "Hey guys," you can hear him say, almost laughingly, "no one who does a deed of power in my name will be able soon afterward to speak evil of me. Grace is irresistible. This fellow is with us. Encourage his faith, and be open to the surprises he may bring to you. Welcome him, like I told you to welcome a child. Treat him gently...treat him with respect."

It seems to me that there is a very strange mystery enshrouded here in a most mundane encounter. What Jesus sees is reality—what we see is some carved-down, lint-sized sliver of reality. The familiar makes us comfortable; the strange and mysterious sends up our antennae. Yet it is always in the stranger—in the unexpected and the unanticipated—that the mystery and presence of God can be seen. Who would ever have thought up a crucifixion on a lonely hill as a way for God to tell us about himself and us?

I think there is, deep beneath this story of the disciples' encounter with a stranger, a profound biblical theme: Jesus is the great and profound respecter of persons. He sees something good in you that you don't see in yourself. He sees something good in others that you don't see in them. He invites his disciples, and he invites you, to see in that particular stranger a fellow struggler in the faith, perhaps one simply caught up in the mystery.

And then there is the last line of this story that I first read this way: "For truly I tell you, the one to whom you give a cup of water to drink, because you bear the name of Christ, will by no means lose the reward." But that's not how it reads! You see, I am expecting Jesus to be full of all this moralizing about life. Rather it says, "Whoever gives you a cup of water to drink, because you bear the name of Christ, will by no means lose the reward."

Grace comes from strangers, and such strangers are even graced. Grace comes from the unlikely—perhaps even the unfaithful. What a big and mysterious God we have, who turns reality upside down, every time we think we have it nailed down on a cross, or boxed up and tied securely with ribbons, or slammed shut in a tomb with a big stone rolled in front of it.

Two disciples were walking down the road to Emmaus, discussing the sad things that had happened the two previous days since the crucifixion. And a stranger (Jesus) came up to them and joined them in their journey. There it is—it happened again—grace in the stranger. Then there is the first apostle in the Christian movement: a woman who had five husbands—a stranger whom Jesus met at a well—and there it is again. And then there is Jesus himself, the world's perennial stranger. He was in the world, and the world came into being through him; yet the world did not know him. And there is it again!

Perhaps, even today, you will encounter a stranger. At the bus stop. In the coffee shop. Stalled by the side of the road in an overheated vehicle. Seated on a bench, dressed in a tattered coat and feeding the birds from a grease-stained paper bag. My friend, meet the grace of God.

Chapter 33
Regaining the Gift of Our Humanity

James and John, known as "sons of thunder," for their boisterous and aggressive ways, step forward, grab Jesus by the arm, and say to him, "Teacher, we want you to do for us whatever we ask you."

You've heard that kind of question before, haven't you? And up went your antennae. It's kind of a trap question. If the person says okay, then you can control them—you can tell them to stand on their head, hold this snake, or have them give you fifty dollars.

That the sons of thunder asked Jesus this question tells us more about them: they wanted to get control of Jesus and squeeze something out for their own personal need. Jesus caught the thrust of their question and replied wisely, "Come on, guys, tell me first what you want me to do for you." You couldn't put anything over on this young rabbi!

And they said to Jesus, "Grant us to sit, one at your right hand and one at your left, in your glory." Now if there is only one spot at the right and only one spot at the left, what about those other ten fellows who were also Jesus's friends? Where would they sit—at the feet of this trio? Now they weren't saying that Jesus had to set up this new arrangement right away—only when he was "in his glory."

But what was his glory? My New Testament instructor in Divinity School, who himself was Jewish, said "in his glory" meant that James and John expected Jesus to wallop the hell out of the Gentiles, kick out the Romans, set up a throne in Jerusalem with an advisor on the right and an advisor on the left, pay a minimum wage to everyone and a maximum wage to James and John, cut taxes, reduce crime on the road to Jericho, and let everyone live happily ever after with their daily entitlements of chocolate ice cream. So goes the Doctrine of Glory, according to James and John. It is, of course, defective, even though much of religion has always worshiped and yearned for this god, especially today.

Jesus came into his glory when he died, stripped naked of every possession, with a thief on the right and a thief on the left. The glory of God was the grief and love felt by a Father when he beheld his only son in anguish, giving selflessly his last bit of human energy in a failing campaign of grace. God's power was in God's utter weakness. God's glory was in his utter debasement and shame, nailed to a cross on a hill, away from civilization.

So Jesus said to James and John, "You do not know what you are asking. Are you able to drink the cup I drink and be baptized with my baptism?"

They replied, "We are able!" Sure we can, Jesus. We know how it will all turn out.

Do you remember the devil's three temptations of Jesus in the desert? Satisfy their hunger, and you will rule. Throw yourself down from a pinnacle, and God will take care of you. Look at all this power in these kingdoms, I will give them to you, Jesus. This is what is in the heads of the sons of thunder—a total misunderstanding and a complete twisting of the glory of God.

What has gone wrong here? What is this power grab by James and John all about? What are they really trying to pull off here, in this rather desperate and unseemly exchange with the man who had told them three times that his fate was a shameful encounter with a cross?

Understanding this is critical, because I think it reveals the crucial issue in the Church of Jesus Christ today. This is what unconsciously drives the dreams of religious people today. James and John want to be gods. It's that simple—and it is what they view a god to be: all powerful, seated with Jesus above the others, while their ten friends curl up at their feet. James and John despise their humanity! They want to be gods. Being human is hateful.

My beloved friend, Brennan Manning, a Roman Catholic evangelist, said time and again in his books and his preaching and counseling, that he is overwhelmed, as he travels the circuit today, by the amount of self-hatred he sees in people—and how self-destructive it is. No wonder we want to be gods. So much of our life's course is devoted to becoming part of the pantheon of immortal gods. This is not the cheap theologizing of learning to like oneself. No, this is a profound wrestling with the first commandment. The sin most deeply exposed in the modern world is our will to be gods, in response to the self-hatred of our humanity. We do not like how God has put us together, so we will change it. No, that's not quite it. In reality, in spite of the polls, humankind hardly shows signs of belief that there even is a god who gave us our humanity as a gift. Hence, we must create ourselves in the images of our god.

There is one person, among a few in Christian history, who has understood that God does not make us gods, nor can we make ourselves gods. His name was Martin Luther. Luther was one of the few who grasped that the cross of Jesus meant that God delighted in giving us back our humanity in which to rejoice and revel. God liked what he saw in the human enterprise of Jesus. God yearned that we be what he created us to be: human beings, God's partners in creation, walking hand in hand with one another in the cool of the evening in a garden, chatting about life with our creator.

And in the cross of Jesus, God has given us back our humanity. He has given us a human friend in whom the fullness of God is touched and felt, or as the Book of Hebrews says, "A great high priest who can sympathize with our weaknesses..."

We make mistakes...but we are forgiven. We face death...but it has no sting. We may suffer, but nothing can separate us from the love of him who suffered the deepest loss. In a beloved hymn, death is even regarded as a friend, most kind and gentle. Now walk into a modern hospital today and tell me if death is seen as a friend, kind and gentle. Tell me what it is that we worship.

There is another great hymn that the Christian community sings at Easter: "The Strife Is O'er, the Battle Done." The strife is over! God has restored our humanity. We can love without self-interest, we can play with abandonment, we can work with dedication, sharing with our Creator his love for his precious creation.

Jesus said to James and John: You will drink my cup, but no human being—not even I—can give you back your humanity. Only our Father can do that, from the depths of his loving heart, in this place he has prepared for you.

No more do we need to be caught in the embarrassing position of James and John, trying to get control of our human situation and making foolish requests of Jesus and his Father, and making everybody else quite angry. If only those two fellows had known what Jesus was going to do for them without their asking.

Our Father, who is in heaven, and whose name we hallow, has given us back our humanity—to cherish, to enjoy, to love and serve. We are free to be human. And may our thunder be turned into gentle rains that nourish the seeds of life, germinating in the soil of God's good creation.

Chapter 34
God's Defining Moment on the Cross

*I*n our lives there are what we call defining moments. A defining moment in life is that very brief occasion when a decision is made, or when an event happens, that shapes the rest of your life and either gives it meaning or wrenches from it the last shred of meaning. Perhaps you have been through such a defining moment in your life. Maybe you finally got up the courage to ask the woman of your dreams if she would marry you. How long does it take to ask that question? Suddenly, once uttered, life is never the same. And perhaps you were foolish enough, in an even briefer span of time to reply, "Why of course—I hoped you'd ask." And life has never been the same.

Or maybe you once took a trip to a desperately poor country. You lingered there a while, observing the means by which many of the people of this earth subsist. All your carefully constructed career goals evaporated, and life has never been the same for you.

It is as if all of life hangs in the balance at that defining moment. Everything is suspended, until the moment passes, and a risky journey down a new road is launched.

Such is the Festival of Christ the King. It is that strange day in the liturgical calendar that concludes the church year every autumn with the daring confession, before a power-thirsty world, that the king reigns from the tree! The crown of glory is infested with thorns. The jewels and gems of the king are his wounds. The king's army is recruited from a hapless band of lovers. His weapon of conquest is self-sacrificial love proclaiming that all of his dying soldiers on life's battlefields will taste life again.

Today the world is turned upside down—indeed, turned inside out—to reveal its king and the real power behind the throne. This is the man of the cross in whom the face of God is finally seen in all its glorious beauty.

Pontius Pilate had a defining moment in his life, which he never recognized, when he stared at the fragile frame of an obscure Galilean rabbi. Pontius was simply doing his job, earning his keep, trying to manage the economy and keep the peace in an occupied land. Pretenders to power, as is always the case, were a dime a dozen. Here was another, a man beaten and humbled, betrayed and forgotten, standing before him in judgment. Or was it Pilate who was being judged by this hapless warrior of God?

"Are you the King of the Jews?" Pontius asks. I wonder in what tone of voice he asked God that question—for Jesus's reply is utterly stunning. His words precipitate, for Pontius, a defining moment in life. "Do you ask this on your own?" inquires Jesus, as if Jesus is reaching out to him toward his heart, offering him the peace which Pontius's power cannot give him. "Or did others tell you about me?" asks Jesus, inviting Pilate to open his heart to God's warm embrace. What would have happened, if Pilate had answered God's probing questions at this defining moment? Sad to say, Pilate ducked the questions of this defining moment and chose politics instead.

Not infrequently, I think of one of my friends who did not avoid life's defining moment. Robab Lordgooee, a mother from Shiraz, Iran, was visiting her daughter in the United States. One day, Robab came to me saying, in hardly discernible English, "I want to be baptized." I agreed to baptize her. After her baptism, she confided her dreadful dilemma to me. When she returned home, if anyone learned of her baptism, she would have two choices. She could renounce her Christian faith in the public square...or she would be summarily executed, like her Lord and King.

Few, if any of us, have such defining moments in our lives as Pilate and Robab, moments when the human face of God probes so deeply into the human heart. C.S. Lewis, that most practical and insightful exponent of the Christian, faith speaks of our defining moments before our King in his book, *Mere Christianity*. Lewis suggests that, for most of us, the defining moments of our lives come the very moment when we wake up each morning. The moment when we shut off the alarm, stagger from our slumber, grab the newspaper and begin pumping caffeine into our stomachs. The moment when we truly awaken, and all the wishes and demands of the day begin to rush in like wild animals, provoking our anxieties.

The first task, Lewis insists, is that we shove them all back, and then listen to that other voice. He urges us to allow the larger, stronger, quieter life to come flowing into us. To let Christ, the gentle king, rule the day with us. He implores us to let each day begin with a defining moment with the God who reigns from the tree. Rather than rush on anxiously to the hairdryer and the shaving cream, let our world be turned upside down, to reveal the suffering love who is in charge of all of this, a love that assures us, by the king's woundedness, that God is indeed one with us.

Chapter 35
Why?

Some years ago, I was returning rather late one evening from a class at the university. When I arrived home, I received the message that something had happened to one of my parishioners—a teen-ager whom I had confirmed two years earlier. When I arrived at his home and met his mother, her face contorted in pain, I knew what had happened. He had committed suicide. She cried out, "Why?" I stood there mute...shaken...and I held her.

Two months later, I received a call about midnight. A nine-year-old child of one of my parishioners had died in his mother's arms of a cardiac seizure as he gleefully jumped off an amusement ride at Opryland.

Eight days later, as I entered my office one morning, the phone rang. It was a call from the emergency room of one of the hospitals. A popular and delightful teenager in the congregation—a championship swimmer—had been in an auto accident and was permanently paralyzed from the waist down.

And all of them wondered what I am sure many of us have wondered—how can this be? How can God allow such unwarranted suffering? How can God permit such tragedy, tragedy which we witness almost daily? And people cry out for an answer, trying to make some sense out of something that seems utterly senseless.

Many times during those painful four months, I found myself standing there, often mute, unable to unlock the answer to life's most painful question. All I could do was hold my parishioners, catch their tears, and listen to their anger.

Jesus himself encountered this most painful question of life. The gospel tells us how it was posed to Jesus, and how he responded. His answer is sure to shock many of us. Some people came to Jesus who were obviously struggling with this age-old question of evil and unmerited suffering in life. They called his attention to the innocent Galileans, at worship before their God, whom Pilate had slaughtered and mixed their blood with their offerings to God. And Jesus replied, "Do you think that these Galileans were worse sinners than all the other Galileans because they suffered thus in life?" It is such an insensitive way to make sense of the senseless. But such reasoning is often tried in desperation, because we want answers. Maybe they were being punished? Maybe it was the will of God?

Jesus bursts forth, "I tell you, no!" thereby severing any causal connection between unmerited suffering and sin and God. And yet, his answer is like a muted silence. He doesn't offer an answer to their question. He stands there mute, except for what seems to be a caustic addition, "Unless you repent, you will all likewise perish."

He didn't need to say that, did he? That was almost unkind. And he didn't stop there but pushed that repentance business back at them again, "Those eighteen upon whom the tower in Siloam fell and killed them, do you think they were any worse offenders than all the others who dwelt in Jerusalem? I tell you, no! But unless you repent you will all likewise perish."

Jesus could have been a bit more sensitive, but to Jesus all violence and suffering, whether caused by natural disaster or human sinfulness, was evil. Evil is evil, hurt is hurt, suffering is suffering. Jesus knew that such questions and searches for answers often steer us away from the primary question of life.

It is a Lenten question, which is not about life's fairness or unfairness, but rather about how we stand before God. Thus he could risk the unthinkable by responding, unless you repent...unless you turn around and return to God...return home...then you too will perish. These words of invitation are issued by a loving God—a caring Father—urging us to come to our senses and come home to live, and to live selflessly.

For most of us, any suffering or tragedy is patently unfair and undeserved, because we have stopped trusting in a God whose presence makes suffering, confusion, and tragedy bearable. Rather than the dwelling in the mystery of God and his presence, we want answers—neat and clean—so that we can go about our business, rather than risk offering ourselves to others as a sign of God's presence.

Will Willimon, commenting on this dilemma, says, "The notion that only good things happen to good people was put to rest when we hung Jesus on the cross. This same Jesus takes our question about why bad things happen to good people, and makes it cruciform: Can you trust God, in joy and pain, to be your God? Can you let go of your demand that God be a god on your own terms? Can you love God without linking your love to the cards life deals you? God's love carries no promises about good or bad, save the promise that God will not allow anything worse to happen to us than what happened to his own son!"

Moses was basking in suburban luxury in the hills of Midian, effortlessly tending the flocks of his affluent father-in-law, when he inadvertently stumbled onto holy ground. And there he stood, trembling, as his God beckoned him to go down to Egypt to shake his fist at secular power. God's command terrified him, because he knew the risks to his life. God was beckoning him to organize a lovable but cantankerous people for a long trek into the future—which also terrified him, because he knew the risks to his body.

And what did God promise him? This—and only this—to accompany him throughout his life. Turn to me, Moses, and I will be with you. I will be with you.

Ultimately, Jesus himself asked life's unanswerable question. As his life blood drained away, he cried out, interrogating the heavens for everyone, "My God, my God why have you forsaken me?" And then, in his next words, he answered that question in the only way it can be answered, "Father, into your hands I commend my spirit."

Turn to me...return to me...and I will be with you!

Those three dear families? Two of them attend worship regularly...the other still tries.

Turn to me...return to me...and I will be with you!

Chapter 36
And I Will Bear Your Burdens

"Come to me, all you that are weary and are carrying heavy burdens, and I will give you rest. Take my yoke upon you, and learn from experience from me; for I am gentle and humble in heart, and you will discover rest for your souls. For my yoke is easy, and my burden is light"

When Susan and I lived in Namibia, we did not have to travel very far to gain a picture of what Jesus is talking about in the above verse from the Gospel of Matthew. We only needed to go out to the fields where oxen had been pulling the plows—pulling the plows to turn up the ground so that the mahanghu seeds could be planted. Sometimes these oxen were yoked together in order to pull the plow.

The yoke around the necks of these animals is heavy—tiresome—a burden for them to bear. From sunrise to sunset, the heavy burden of the yoke around their necks, the oxen trudge forward, exhausting their strength in the heat of the scorching sun. At the end of each day they plod home, exhausted—drained of all their energy, of all their strength, of their life.

When these oxen labor and struggle to move forward under the burden of the yoke, something interesting is happening. When that yoke is weighing heavily upon the poor oxen's shoulders, they cannot look back to anything. They cannot look to the sides at anything. And because of the weight of the yoke, their heads begin to fall toward the ground. They can see little of anything in front of themselves. With each step they take forward, they see only the ground—the dirt at their feet. They cannot see the past, or look forward to the future, nor share in the rest of life that appears at their sides. They are, in a word—*oppressed*—oppressed by the burdensome yoke that they must bear, day to day. Life is heavy—life is difficult.

The word "yoke" appears sixty-nine times in the Bible. In every situation except one, the word is used as a symbol of oppression—a symbol of being burdened—a symbol of suffering in life. A yoke is a symbol of being harnessed, trapped, weighed down by life's burdens and the pain of living that accompanies such bearing of burdens.

So when Jesus looks out at the crowds gathered around him, he sees the depth of their oppression in life. And his heart aches in compassion for his people. He uses this image of the yoke, the burden of the oxen, as a sign to them that he sees their exhaustion with trying to live—trying to survive. He sees into the souls that are wounded and without hope for a future beyond the burdens of this day. The heart of Jesus—the heart of God—reaches out in deep compassion for all the burdens you bear, for all the burdens which exhaust and drain your life of rest, beauty, and joy. God did not intend for human beings to be yoked and burdened. He did not intend for you to be oppressed.

There is no one reading this who does not bear a burden. Some of you bear burdens that are very heavy. We all labor under the burden that we will die. We all have lived under the burden of illness, whether our own or the illness of someone we loved. Many know the burdens of being unemployed, of struggling endlessly to find some food for children or the aged and disabled. Some bear the burden of guilt. Some bear the burden of betrayal. Some bear the burden of failure. Some bear the burden of addiction. We have labored in life—and we are weary from its burdens.

Is there any hope for life to be otherwise? For our lives to be different?

Jesus says to you today—right now, *to you*—the same thing he said to the crowds whom he saw yoked by their burdens, "Come to me—all you that are weary—and are carrying heavy burdens—and I will give you rest—I will refresh you—I will give you hope—I will share your burdens—lift you up—and give you strength. I will hold you in my arms and give you comfort."

In speaking to the deepest burden we bear in life—our own dying and our own fear of death—Jesus, the Resurrected Lord of Life, says, "Have no fear—in me you shall live. Nothing in life—not even death—can separate you from the loving arms of my Father."

No longer do you and I live under the yoke of death or the burden of fearing death. We have been freed from that burden which cuts off the future, and, having been so freed, we can be people of hope. We can be people of courage, people of daring, people of risk We can dare to believe that this little, precious life of ours can be less burdened. That the yokes of life that enslave and oppress can finally be broken.

The voice of Jesus still cries out today for justice, for food for the hungry, for medical care for the ailing, for compassion for the guilty and broken-hearted. The voice of Jesus still cries out for freedom from life's burdens across the plains of Africa and the deserts of the Middle East, across the prairies of Kansas and the streets of Chicago.

Who will take up that voice—proclaim rest and refreshment in God—hope and healing in Jesus? Who will speak the Word of God that lifts the yoke and frees God's creation from oppression? Will you?

Chapter 37
I Judge No One

A number of years ago Martin Buber, a well-known Jewish theologian, wrote a little book that bore the fascinating title, *The Eclipse of God*. His main point in this book was that the reality of God in the 20th century (and, we might add, the 21st century) had become hidden from sight, the same way the warmth of the sun is hidden in the process of a solar eclipse. What fascinates me about Buber's little book is the picture that his title so graphically conveys. Perhaps we can use this image of an eclipse as a way of understanding this meditation.

One day, during the time that Susan and I were teaching in Namibia, about one o'clock in the afternoon, everyone in the country witnessed here a near total eclipse of the sun. Our neighbors in Angola, Zambia, and Zimbabwe witnessed a total eclipse. Our African students, although they were all young, educated adults, became worried. Slowly and gradually our world began to darken in the middle of the day. What had been a reasonably warm afternoon became cool and chilly as the light of the sun dimmed. And no matter how sophisticated they thought they were in understanding an eclipse of the sun, no matter that they knew the light and warmth would soon return, they had an eerie fear that maybe this was what it would be like when the end came and the sun never returned.

An eclipse is so easy to understand. As the moon orbits around the earth and the earth orbits around the sun, there is a point and a time when the moon blocks the warm rays of the sun's light. When that happens, the warm and radiant sunlight that bathes the earth is dimmed, eclipsed, hidden from sight. A part of the earth becomes darker, colder, and eerier as the moon hides the reality of the sun and the rays of light and warmth. It is an eclipse!

Now suppose that we substitute for the sun, God. And suppose that we substitute something for the moon—it doesn't matter what—that comes between God and us. Then, might not we have what Buber was referring to in the title of his little book, *The Eclipse of God*? The reality of the divine would be hidden from us.

Let us further suppose that we took seriously the simple yet powerful words of the first epistle of John: "Whoever does not love, does not know God—for *"God is love!"* Then what is eclipsed—hidden from sight and reality—is the radiant, life-giving and soul-warming love of the divine, a love that is pure compassion and grace. When the God who is love is eclipsed, then life becomes darker, colder and eerier, and filled with fear.

Israel's religious authorities brought to Jesus a woman—they dragged her to him—holding her tightly in their grip. They thrust the woman before Jesus, and then they stood back from, her at a distance, for fear that she might contaminate them. One of their esteemed group announced, "This woman was caught in the very act of adultery." Interestingly, we may note, the man who also participated in this act of adultery is ignored by the authorities—we hear nothing of him. Maybe he ran faster than she did. Or maybe these authorities are made bold in their weakness before this helpless woman.

Standing there, righteously and rigidly, they remind Jesus that the Law of Moses requires that she be stoned to death—her life destroyed—and they begin to search in the dirt for their weapons of execution. In that very moment, God who is love is eclipsed. Life is dark, cold and filled with fear on that morning. The eclipse of God—the eclipse of love—threatens to unleash violence and destruction of life. Such things happen when the God who is love is eclipsed.

That morning, legalism, judgmentalism, and fear eclipse the grace and compassion of love. They render life dark and violent. It is easy to see that the source of the eclipse of God are the very religious authorities themselves. They represent a religious stance in which legalism and judgmentalism shrink religion itself into a life-destroying force.

Jesus bends down and writes something in the sand at their feet. What do you suppose he wrote? But, still, they keep pressing him aggressively as if he is the real enemy. And then he shocks them, "Let anyone among you who is without sin be the first to throw a stone at her." Throw a stone and kill her! And again he writes something in the sand. What do you suppose he wrote in the sand? (Could it be, "I judge no one"?) One by one—defeated by the light of life—they slink off into their own personal darkness.

There Jesus stands, alone with the woman. Radiating, in indescribable brilliance, the compassion of God, he asks, "Who condemns you my sister?"

"No one," she replies.

"Nor do I," says Jesus. Nor do I.

The God who is love—the reality of love—no longer is eclipsed, but is shining in all his brilliance and all his life-giving and life-affirming love.

In the verses that follow this near eclipse of God, Jesus describes himself, not surprisingly, as the light of the world. He is that very radiant, life-giving love that lightens the darkness of this world and the evil ways of our own hearts. And then he says what must be one of the most shocking statements in all the scriptures. Jesus says, *"I judge no one."* No one!

When the eclipse of God has passed, what are we to do with these shocking words? The manifestation of God-as-love says, "I judge no one." Why, then, does one hear so much judgment spoken in communities of the followers of Christ? Why is pure grace eclipsed and hidden from the sight of those who hunger for the warmth of love? What is it inside of us that, even in spite of our best attempts at discipline, finds us judging others? Why do we eclipse them, by our own darkness, from the radiant love that is the essence of the divine? And why do some of us justify the darkness of that judging by appeals to religion, especially when the Light of the World stands before the religious authorities and announces, *"I judge no one"*?

What a profoundly radical religion we profess to participate in. Its cornerstone says, "I judge no one." If we dare to be obedient to his words, "Follow me," then what new shape might our lives take? Our lives together— our lives in all our relationships? And if his followers dared to be so bold, might not the eclipse of God pass? Might the warm, radiant, life-giving and life-affirming love called "grace" embrace this creation? Might that grace still hearts everywhere, and convince the hungering that nothing—to paraphrase St. Paul—indeed nothing in this life can eclipse us from the love of God in Christ Jesus our Lord?

Chapter 38
The Man Who Had No Name

There was a rich man who was dressed in purple and fine linen and lived in luxury every day. At his gate was laid a beggar named Lazarus, covered with sores and longing to eat what fell from the rich man's table. Even the dogs came and licked his sores. The time came when the beggar died and the angels carried him to Abraham's side. The rich man also died and was buried. In hell, where he was in torment, he looked up and saw Abraham far away, with Lazarus by his side. So he called to him, "Father Abraham, have pity on me and send Lazarus to dip the tip of his finger in water and cool my tongue, because I am in agony in this fire." But Abraham replied, "Son, remember that in your lifetime you received your good things, while Lazarus received bad things, but now he is comforted here and you are in agony. And besides all this, between us and you a great chasm has been fixed, so that those who want to go from here to you cannot, nor can anyone cross over from there to us." He answered, "Then I beg you, father, send Lazarus to my father's house, for I have five brothers. Let him warn them, so that they will not also come to this place of torment." Abraham replied, "They have Moses and the Prophets; let them listen to them." "No, father Abraham," he said, "but if someone from the dead goes to them, they will repent." He said to him, "If they do not listen to Moses and the Prophets, they will not be convinced even if someone rises from the dead."

Luke 16: 19-31

*W*hat do you suppose this story that Jesus told is about? When you read it, you are struck by this tension between the rich and the poor. One aspect of life in southern Africa is the blatant disparity between some of the glittering cities, such as Windhoek, Namibia or Cape Town, South Africa, and the desperately poor "locations," just outside the city. A location is the area where poor, indigenous people live, often in tarpaper shacks and often without electricity or plumbing. If you live in a location, and are fortunate enough to be employed, it is likely as a day laborer or a maid, cook, or gardener for those who live in the city. If you live in one of these cities, you can become blind to this chasm of inequality. It can simply be regarded as the status quo.

When you read this story, you may be tempted to see it as a social justice story that turns the world of the rich upside down, as well as the world of the poor. The story seems to say that those who have suffered in their poverty in this world will be blessed in the next—and those who have enjoyed luxuries in this world will suffer in the next. But is that, really, very comforting or consoling to the poor? To tell them to be patient with their poverty today, because someday, in the next life, they will live in the land of milk and honey? Do I want to wait until the day I die to finally have my hungering stomach filled? Travel to one of those locations with me someday, and deliver that message to those who dwell there. Do you think you would receive a warm reception? It certainly wouldn't be very good news, would it?

Nor would you receive a very warm reception if you told the poor that this is simply the way it is. That, somehow, we are fated by God's will—some to be rich and some to be poor. That's not good news either.

So what is this powerful little story about? What was Jesus getting at, when he told this story? Perhaps, it would help if I reminded you that in the Jewish tradition, in Israel's folk theology, riches were seen as a blessing of God, and that this man's poverty was virtually God's curse upon him. If you did well, you were rewarded with the blessings of God. If you did less well, then you might find yourself a poor one sitting at the beggar's gate. If you were rich, you had excelled—if you were poor you had obviously somehow failed. Well, if that is the case, then a lot of us are in disfavor with God!

Such was the Jewish folk theology—and, unfortunately, that same theology lingers all too often today. But Jesus tells a stunning little story that turns everything upside down. He stands Jewish folk theology on its head with a revolutionary notion. Riches are not necessarily a sign of God's favor or approval, nor even God's blessings. One has to probe deeply into this story to get at what Jesus was saying—namely that he was obliterating folk theology in favor of a new way of seeing and experiencing life under God. Jesus suggests something radically new: *how we relate to one another* determines how we are related to God. This is what shapes our destiny.

Try to visualize this story—as if you were standing there today as a bystander outside the rich man's gate. There was a rich man who was dressed in purple and fine linen and who feasted sumptuously every day—not just on Sundays, but every day of the week. He pulls up in front of his large house, his black Mercedes screeching to a halt. It's been a long day checking out his investments and balancing his many bank accounts. He jumps out of his Mercedes, his sunglasses slightly askew, and he rushes toward the door of his private fortress. The maid tells him that his champagne is chilling, and the steaks are on the grill.

Do you know what that man's name is, by any chance? Does Jesus give him a name in this story? The man has no name—he is a non-person. Because he has no name, you can't relate to him, nor can he relate to others. *His lack of a name suggests that he is somehow not quite human.*

At the gate to his house—which he passes through every day—lies a poor man named Lazarus. Although he is poor, he has a name. He is someone—he is a person. We can relate to him, and he to us. He is not healthy; he is covered with sores. Lazarus yearns—"longs," according to Luke—to satisfy the gnawing hunger with what falls from the rich man's table. Note what the text says, "He longs to satisfy his hunger." But it does not say that he ever gets anything—not even a scrap of garbage. The rich man never stops to acknowledge Lazarus's hunger. He doesn't even drop a few coins in his gnarled hand. Lazarus can only yearn for something to satisfy his hunger—his hunger in life never satisfied.

And what's more, the dogs lick his wounds. The story seems to suggest that this is a horrible thing, but is there another message there? It is the world of the animals who seem to minister to this poor beggar, bringing some comfort, perhaps, to his condition.

But now, you who are watching this story unfold, did you notice something about this rich man when he hurried out of his Mercedes—day after day—rushing into the safety and security of his home? Did you notice that he never sees Lazarus lying there? He never looks at him? The rich man is a non-person who does not see the other person—the one who has a name. He does not see the precious humanity lying at his gate. He is entirely unable to relate to this human being. He cannot see life. And this rich man—who has no name—no identity as a person—pays the high price of torment in terms of his future destiny. The person who has a name—Lazarus—is blessed by Father Abraham, and ultimately you and me…because we know him.

Jesus has turned the world of folk religion upside down by suggesting that our personal destiny is deeply entwined with our personal and social relationships. Do we really see the suffering who lie at our gates, yearning? Do we have eyes of compassion that can see something more than just a sick, hungry old man with scabs and wounds lying there? Can we take off our sunglasses, our blinders, and see our brother, Lazarus, beloved child of God, lying there, yearning for the touch of grace and healing and sustenance?

Jesus teaches us how to peer through the fear and insecurity and self-absorption that strip us of our God-given humanity. He teaches us to perceive the precious human being, the one who has a name and yearns for healing.

Suffering has a name—Lazarus. Sickness has a name—Agnes. Depression has a name—John. Grief has a name—Rene. Alcoholism has a name—Leon. Hunger has a name—Thomas.

If you watch Jesus closely throughout the three brief years of his ministry, he doesn't look away or avoid eye contact with suffering—he joins it, identifies with it, enters into it, embraces it. Those whom the unnamed rich cannot see, Jesus takes by the hand and says, "You are my brother—you are my sister." And the Kingdom of God becomes a fellowship of beggars, and criminals, and marginalized souls, the walking wounded, the poor of the earth, and the lost and forgotten children with Jesus at the center.

Chapter 39
He Knows What It Means To Be Me

*I*t is late afternoon. The shadows are deepening, and the sun prepares to rest after a day's labor through the heavens. You and I are sitting next to one another—high up on this mountain, far above the care and anxieties of the world below us. Down there in the valley people are working hard: straining, stressing, buying, selling, gathering, dealing.

We are not alone on the mountain. There is a vast crowd of people, more than you and I have ever seen gathered in one place, here in Galilee. (Sometimes I am uneasy in such large crowds—I feel as if I lose myself in this mass of humanity.) You and I and this huge crowd (and I don't see a single other familiar face) are sitting here on this mountain. We are listening. Listening to a young man who says he is a rabbi. I don't know him personally—I've never met him, nor run into him at the temple, nor shaken his hand. But we heard that he does wondrous things and speaks with great power. Somehow he seems so close to God—yet so close to life, too, as if he is somehow both human and divine. People have told us that if anyone understands life, he does. He seems to peer into it so deeply and reveal its mystery. So you and I have come to this mountain, and here we sit, listening. We are entranced. He has such power, and he speaks so deeply and truthfully about what we experience. He touches our hearts and steals into the hidden corners of our lives. When we look into his eyes, he looks back as if he has known us all our lives and knows every joy and sorrow and secret that has ever found a home in our hearts.

He's not the most handsome young man we have ever seen. He's so frail and thin. He looks almost weak. And yet, a passionate holiness radiates around him. And did you hear what he just said, "Therefore, I tell you, do not worry about your life...(*Do not worry about my life!*)...what you will eat or what you will drink or about your body, what you will wear..." Does he really mean that? Does he really believe that? Hasn't he looked around at this crowd?

You and I don't have much to call our own. Our clothes, including what we are wearing this afternoon, are rather tattered. And life in this place...well, we have to worry about where our next meal is coming from. We're not like some of those rich folks down there in the valley who not only survive but prosper in all their wheeling and dealing and bargaining and buying. We are the poor of this earth. We scrape by just to survive. We live with worry and anxiety as our daily diet!

But listen to what he is saying to everyone here. He is telling us to look at those little birds flying above our heads, and he is saying that there is, at the center of creation, a power of love that even provides for them. He is saying that you and I are of even more value to this great love.

I don't know about you, but sometimes I feel so worthless—that nobody cares about me, that no one will ever remember me when I am gone, that I am so alone in this universe. But listen: he's saying that there is a love in this whole creation that knows me, loves me and even, mysteriously, will provide for me—if I trust that love. Does he really dare to suggest that we can be care-free?

I don't know about you, but he is starting to reach me. He knows what it means to be human. He knows what it means to be...me. He even knows about that deep dark question that haunts me most—the question I never dare to ask or share with anyone. You and I both know that we must die. That is the fear that stalks me, like the lion his prey. Some of these old folks here on the mountain won't be with us next year. Even some of these young ones here won't be here in a few years. I watch the nightly news and see so many lives ended by evil. My deepest fear, my hidden anxiety, presses me hard to add an hour—a few days—a few years to this fragile life. Is this really *life*, living in such anxiety that we are like grass that springs up green in the spring rain, only to be scorched later into lifelessness and blown away into oblivion like windborne dust?

But he says not to worry—not to be anxious—not to be frightened. Is he actually telling us that we don't have to be worried about our survival—now or ever? He is saying that he has seen the love at the center of creation to which each and every one of us in this crowd is so dear and precious. He is telling us that the name of this love is Abba...Daddy...Father. He seems so confident and certain, doesn't he?

And you and I? He's right—we are so faithless. It is so hard to trust that someone really cares, and that life is indeed more than survival. It is so human to doubt, and often with good reason. But I have never heard someone speak such beautiful and comforting truth with such authority. And look at the astonished faces in this crowd! I can trust him. I never would have thought that I would see the face of God in this strange man—but that's what I see right now. And I hear the voice of a loving Father calling to me to trust, not to be anxious, not to worry, not to be frightened. This must be the peace of God.

You notice, don't you, that the sun is beginning to set. We have to go to our homes soon. Why don't we leave behind the things that worry us? Let's learn from him. Let's watch how he lives his life—and dies his death. He seems so calm and strong, as if nothing can shake him. Let's join him in his quest for the Kingdom of God. Maybe he does have something to teach us.

Look at the feast he has prepared for us who hunger and thirst for life. A little piece of bread, a sip of wine—his body, his blood, his heart and his soul—his promise that love is at the center of the universe. He wants to feed us and sustain us throughout our journey with these assurances that we need not fear. Perhaps we ought to join him at his feast more often, to ease the pain of our hunger and quench our thirst for life.

But now we need to go down from this mountain, back to our valley. You notice, don't you, that the sun has set and darkness has fallen. But look—up at the sky—the stars are shining. There is light in our darkness. We need not fear.

Chapter 40
Another Way of Living In The World

You shall love the Lord your God with all your heart, and with all your soul, and with all your mind and with all your strength. The second is this, You shall love your neighbor as yourself.

*H*ow many times have we heard this spoken in church life, taught in church life, preached in church life? We have heard it so many times that we do not really hear it anymore. We have become numb to the commandments' world-shaking meaning and power. The words fall easily from our mouths: love the Lord your God and love the one next to you, as you love yourself. So numb have we become, so deafened are we to the explosiveness of these words, that we live as if the commandments read this way: "If you have the chance, and the opportunity presents itself, you might try liking the Lord your God with what you have leftover of yourself at the end of a hard day's work or a sleepless night. AND, or by the way, your brother or sister can at times be quite likeable, and if you have the chance, then you might be kindly disposed towards them as you sometimes care about yourself (and of course you do have to look out for number one). But don't become too involved—don't love too deeply—you might get hurt!"

Yet Jesus roars and pleads across Palestine, "Hear, O People of God, an alternative way to live in this dying world! Hear, O People of God, another way to live life in the midst of the empire that smothers hope, denies dignity, and uses peoples' dreams and aspirations for the ease of the empire!"

Out of this empire of legalism in which we all live, out of this empire that can hardly tolerate the radical disruption of its numbed life or the undermining of its values by a community of love, Jesus calls forth the life of a new community. Taking the great commandment from Deuteronomy and unearthing from obscurity the commandment from Leviticus, Jesus combines them into an explosively new way of living together with God, with one another, and, especially, with yourself. Jesus dares to invite you to surrender—to abandon—all the assumptions most dear to you. To relinquish the assumptions that the empire says are the truth, in order to live together as an outpost of grace and forgiveness in the midst of this empire of self-interest.

The empire used the cross to punish and crush a radical lover and maintain the numbing order. God used the cross of Jesus to reveal what it means to live tenderly and compassionately, in relationship with God and one another and ourselves.

Jesus commended the scribe for his wisdom in seeing that the law of love transcended all the old religious sacrifices, but somehow the scribe had not yet fully penetrated the mystery. Jesus says to him, "You are not far off from the kingdom of God—not far off—so near, so close, yet not quite there.

What more could Jesus have been pointing to? What more must be breathed into this commandment to give it its explosive power to transform life from the numbing legalism of the empire? I suggest to you that until you have heard, deep in our own heart, the tenderness of God's compassion and the fullness of God's grace, you cannot begin to love God...or others...or yourself. Until you have accepted this grace in your own heart, you will continue to hate God, despise the other, and be disgusted with yourself.

There is a voice deep inside you. Only you hear it. This is the voice that may speak to you from your family. This is the voice that questions your own self-worth. This is the voice that condemns you for your failure to please others or live up to their expectations. This is the voice that shatters your self-esteem. The voice sows the deepest doubts about yourself, and brings you crashing upon the shores of self-hatred. You cry out, "Who can love me for who I am? Who can love me? Is there a love that vast, that immense, that tender?"

The scribe perceived the distance between himself and the kingdom, the distance between himself and his God, the distance between his neighbor and himself. What he had yet to behold was that the distance has been bridged by Jesus's sacrifice of himself.

Another voice speaks from the cross into your frightened heart. This is the voice from eternity, beyond all the powers of the empire, and this voice whispers: I love you. You belong to me. I esteem you. Nothing you are, and nothing you have done, can ever separate me from you. You are priceless, and today is the first day of your new life.

When you have heard these words from the cross, and when you have taken these words into your body and soul through the sacred meal of our Lord, you become a friend of God. You become a lover of those who, like you, are broken by the inner voice that condemns. Then the hatred of yourself, which you project onto others, is dissolved by the vastness of that love which affirms your infinite worth. You are one with one another and one with God. Together we become a little fellowship in the midst of the empire that reveals a new way to order our lives, order the church, and order the world.

Chapter 41
The Sound in A Thin Silence

*T*he story of Elijah is a parable for our times. Elijah was God's prophet, but during one point in his life he showed all the signs and symptoms of acute clinical depression. He asked the compelling question that sometimes haunts each of us: is it worth it? He turns to his spiritual reservoir, but it is empty. He is spiritually depleted. Maybe these kinds of things happen to ordinary people, but how could this have happened to a prophet of God? One whom God had chosen? His prayer to the Lord had become: O Lord, take away my life. It is all the more baffling, since this depressed prophet of God had just enjoyed one of the most stunning religious successes in Israel's history.

Some background: Ahab, king of the Northern Tribes of Israel, had married Jezebel, a foreigner. Jezebel brought with her, her god Baal. Quickly, Israel's religion was flooded and overwhelmed by the alien gods and their values. Israelites who were itching for something more in life were bowing and kneeling at the altar of Baal.

Elijah challenged this pollution and corruption of Israel's unique and sacred relationship to the true God. He squared off against his culture's atheism, secularism, and corruption of the truth. He challenged four hundred prophets of Baal to a contest to see whether Baal or the Lord God could perform a miracle. An altar to Baal and an altar to the Lord God were built, with a bull carved up for sacrifice on each altar. Then Elijah said to the prophets of Baal, "You call on your god—I'll call on the Lord God; the god who answers by fire is indeed God!"

The prophets of Baal shuffled around the altar, calling out to Baal. No voice answered, and nothing happened. Elijah had made his challenge even more difficult by dousing the altar with water and filling a trench full of water around the altar. He called out to the Lord, "Let your people know that you are the true God!" and the fire came down, consumed the offering and even evaporated the water. That day the people of God were stunned. They rose up and slew the four hundred prophets of Baal.

Elijah seemed to have been a stunning success—he and all the people were in awe at all the glitz and wonder of this spiritually triumphant moment. The choirs rang out. The stringed instruments strummed. The drums beat. No

103

faith-healer had ever enjoyed such success. But Jezebel, infuriated, put a death sentence on Elijah, and Elijah fled to the desert for his life.   But now, strangely, Elijah was depressed. This apparent religious success had yielded only a spiritual emptiness. Do you suppose that this is a warning to us "religious moderns" that all the religious glitz in churches leads ultimately to a spiritual desert?

Elijah is frightened, exhausted, and depleted. He is tired of all this Lord's work business. He is wondering if it's all worth it, because he thinks he is the only one who cares. He cannot even eat—an angel must hand feed him. He falls asleep to rest his weary soul only to be awakened, as if in a hospital, by an angelic nurse, urging him to take sustenance. Finally he arises and walks slowly away until he reaches a cave on Horeb, where he collapses, wrapped in a blanket, waiting for the Lord to grant his wish to die. But Horeb is another name for Mount Sinai, where Moses first received the Ten Commandments. Here in this cave the spiritually dying Elijah is about to encounter the living God. Is there room for you and me to huddle together in Elijah's cave?

And then it happens. He hears a voice, "What are you doing here, Elijah?" Elijah whimpers, in self-pity and loneliness, "I'm the only one, Lord, who cares!" And then it really happens. The Lord says, "Step out here, Elijah, and let me teach you something!" With all the glitz and wonder worthy of Cecil B. DeMille and all the televangelists combined, suddenly, a roaring wind splits the very mountains, creating not a dust storm, but a storm of rocks and boulders. But the Lord is not in the wind! And then an earthquake shakes the foundations of the cave in which Elijah had been hiding. But the Lord was not in the earthquake. And then a roaring fire with a blast of heat sears Elijah's blanket. But the Lord was not in the fire.

And then, the Bible says, there is "a still small voice." That is not a good translation of the Hebrew. Rather, "and then *a thin silence*." A thin silence— not a sound—but thin. Somehow, this is a silence that is pregnant with meaning. You have known that silence. Not the rustle of a leaf, nor the breaking of a twig, nor the splashing of a raindrop on the parched earth. It is a thin silence that is mysteriously full and about to give birth to some new word, some new meaning. In the silence of life comes the moment of revelation.

A voice speaks, and it is the voice of God, breaking his silence. A voice speaks, with brilliant therapeutic insight, to this depressed person, "Elijah, get down off this holy mountain! Go back down into that human melting pot of my beloved people, with all their tangled loyalties and relationships, and get to work! I will go with you and you will know my nearness to you because that is where I am to be found. And get busy loving my beloved humanity."

Well. Not in the glitz, the miraculous, or the wondrous did Elijah encounter the source of his spirituality, but rather somewhere between a "thin silence," where the word can be heard, and the noise of human reality. Perhaps the real spiritual question for us to ask in the midst of *our* thin silence is this: what does it mean to be human? Not the almighty...but simply human. Can we actually believe and trust that salvation can come through the truly human? Through the lives we live, however broken?

Richard Lischer, a Lutheran professor of preaching at Duke Divinity School, has written a wonderful little book entitled, *Open Secrets: A Spiritual Journey through a Country Church*. It is the story of his first ministry as a pastor in a parish of country folk in rural Illinois. A comment by Barbara Brown Taylor on the dust-jacket says of this book: "Lischer tells the truth...how love is hardest among those who are bound together by it, how faith in God offers no protection from loss...and how ordinary people save each other's lives by their simple willingness to be human."

What does it mean to be human? What did Elijah learn in the cave at Horeb? John answers that in the first chapter of his gospel: After the thin silence of many ages, in the pregnant fullness of time, the WORD became flesh and lived among us, full of grace and beauty and truth. Jesus is the essence of being human. Through our ordinary, often unrecognized, acts of compassion and forgiveness, the salvation of God draws near.

You and I can walk out of that cave, get off the mountain, and continue to enter deeply into the reality of our lives. But before we leave the mountain, let us heed the words of the Psalmist: *Be still, and know that I am God.*

Chapter 42
Crosses of Life, Planted Deep in Dust

*W*e *are in bondage to sin and cannot free ourselves.* Thus people in the Christian tradition confess each Sunday morning about our shared human condition. So close is this sin to us that it adheres to our skin like Super Glue, and the glue is both invisible and too strong for us to break. We cannot even see it! Human beings are in bondage, curved in upon themselves. We are not free. That's a radical thing to acknowledge, kneeling in penitence, in this culture that glorifies our supposed autonomy.

"Remember that you are dust and to dust you will return." What a stinging reminder that the sweetness of life ends...in a vault. What a radical confession to make in this culture that denies death. To sit in a pew on Ash Wednesday and agree that human reality is best viewed as being in bondage to sin and returning to dust is culturally heretical. Such a confession is both subversive of a culture that denies death and subversive of a church that worships the comfort of the "massage" rather than the power of the message. But the pews in churches all over the world on Ash Wednesday are reserved for subversives...for honest and heart-aching people who have, simply and wisely, given up on themselves and turned to God.

The Day of Ashes is a solemn and somber day, beginning a long, Lenten stretch of forty days that engages, sometimes painfully, with our inadequacies. But what if the Day of Ashes were seen also as the first day of a season of grace and hope for us subversives? What if we saw the cross of ashes as a symbol of grace, the dawning of hope? What if we viewed this whole season as the advent of ultimate joy? What if we truly repented? Let me explain what I mean.

During Lent, and on the Day of Ashes, you may find yourself overwhelmed with your own sinfulness and guilt. It isn't pretty—perhaps it is frighteningly ugly. And then, kneeling penitently before the altar, you hear these devastating words: *Remember you are dust and to dust you shall return.* Shades of punishment from an angry father. Do you remember where those words came from? They are from the book of Genesis, spoken by God to Adam and Eve after their rebellious act and their exile from Eden. We have always heard this distressing reminder, "Remember you are dust," as some kind of condemnation, a humiliating reminder that we are finite, limited, creatures headed into the abyss of death. We're just dust. *Poof,* and we are scattered into oblivion.

But dust is mentioned even earlier in the Book of Genesis. In that earlier instance there is no judgment upon our being dusty. God takes dust in his hand and breathes life into it. God creates us, delightfully so and in the image of himself. There is nothing wrong with being dusty as long as you don't forget it. Actually, the word in Hebrew is "soil." We are soil. "Remember that you are soil and to soil you shall return."

But we have forgotten that. We get frightened and devote our life project to being something other, seeking to transcend our dustiness, our creaturehood, our finiteness, our death. When we install ourselves as creator—as creator of ourselves—we shove God aside and replace the divine with ourselves, hoping that we can overcome our situation. And when we do that, we destroy ourselves, our relationships, and the natural world.

Yes, we have sinned, and there is virtually only one sin, which cascades into the multiplicity of sins. Anyone who has read the Old Testament soon realizes that all sin hinges upon the first commandment. When we deny our creaturehood, our dependence, our finiteness, all hell breaks loose in our lives. We attempt to take upon our lonely selves the terrifying burden of being our own creators. That is the mess we precipitate every waking morning.

But what if you simply returned to your God with all your heart? What if you admitted you are finite? What if you gave God the burden of being creator and accepted your creaturehood, your dustiness, your very self? What beautiful news! You would no longer feel burdened by being the creator. You can be the creature. Your destiny is given as a gift—not earned, not merited, not by getting life right, not by being in control, not by playing charades and trying to be something you are not.

The cross of ashes begs you to remember that you are a creature, embraced by a love that will not let you go back to the decaying soil. It is the cross of Jesus smudged upon your forehead, that reminds you that you are a creature of a loving, divine power. You can risk being only human. You can rejoice in being a creature. Life can be good! Yes, indeed, Ash Wednesday, is a day of grace and the first planting in the soil of hope. So let your Lenten journey begin on this joyful note:

We are creatures, not creators.
Not foolish fabricators of our destiny, but recipients of a priceless
destiny.
Human, rather than burdened with divinity.

Safe in dependence, rather than driven to despair in independence.
Lovers of others, rather than haters of ourselves.

We are woven and knit into a community of faithful concern, rather than strangers on a lonely trek to the grave. We find our true selves as the image of God, under the tree, at the foot of cross where God's eternal symbol of hope is planted in our decaying soil. Creatures, rejoice in this wondrous creator!

Chapter 43
Dialogue with the Divine

A few years ago I faced the challenge of preaching to a group of seminary students on the Biblical story about a rich man, his abundance of grain, and his dilemma about where to store this windfall gain. These were African students...so poor that neither they nor any family member could pay their minimal school fees. It was a time of drought in northern Namibia—no one had an abundance of grain that year. In truth, no one ever had an abundance. How dare I speak to them of Jesus's warning about greed?

Some years later, the story of this rich man appeared again as the Gospel lesson for me to preach upon. I found myself in a totally different context. It was a context of considerable abundance and affluence. But, again, the lesson surprisingly did not seem to fit the context. I was standing before a group of extraordinarily generous people who had shared greatly. How dare I speak to these people about Jesus's warning on greed?

Perhaps this story, which Jesus tells to the young man in the crowd, is about something more than greed? Perhaps there is something even more significant that lies behind the apparent greed of the rich man, something that is the real danger facing us, no matter what our personal financial condition. Let's try to peel back the layers in this story.

Someone from a crowd asks Jesus to settle a family dispute by asking the man's brother to share the family inheritance. A reasonable and just request, right? After all, Jesus talked a great deal about sharing. But Jesus wisely avoids this request for family intervention. Old Testament law prescribes that the largest portion of an estate pass on to the eldest son. Now that sounds unfair, but there was a reason for this law. The law preserved land in larger tracts for more successful and productive farming. Everyone in society would benefit from this prescription. This man is asking Jesus to overthrow this wise law for his own personal benefit.

So Jesus perceives the man's greed—his request for more than what he was safely entitled to receive. Jesus warns him of his greed and tells him a story which presses deeper into the human heart to describe a very dangerous spiritual condition.

The land of a rich man produced abundantly. Note: it was the *land* that produced the abundance—not the rich man. And as the land produced, the man tore down his smaller barns and built larger and larger barns to store up the wealth that would secure his future. He is blind to the world's suffering. Finally, he can say these supposedly comforting words to himself, "Soul, finally, you have enough for many years to come—relax now. Eat and drink and certainly be merry and whoop it up!"

But who is this rich man talking to? In the short space of three sentences in this Biblical story, he uses the first person singular pronoun eleven times. *I* will store all *my* grain and *my* goods and *I* will say to *my* soul…" This man is talking to himself—babbling to himself. No one is listening. He is imprisoned inside himself. He has no relationship to reality.

In the story, God comes to him in the night, just as the man has achieved his comfort zone, and says, "You fool—it's all over! Tonight your soul—your life—is required of you, and you have nothing to show for your life!"

Perhaps you remember that, in the Sermon on the Mount, Jesus said, "Call no one a fool." To do so is grounds for relentless punishment. What's so bad about calling someone a fool? The first verse of Psalm 14 answers that: "The fool says in his heart: *there is no God!*" The man in Jesus's story is judged by God to be an atheist. He is in dialogue with no one. He has no relationships, no God, no community. He is isolated from all that makes for real life.

The rich man is spiritually bankrupt. Rather than dialogue with God, he charts his life in a self-contained monologue. Little does he realize that his life is already a living hell, for paradise is living in dialogue with the divine and in relationship to other people. Paul Neuchterlein, a Lutheran pastor, suggests that we need to see this story of the rich man's monologue in the context of two other stories about what it means to be human and in dialogue with the divine. In Genesis, "paradise" is described as Adam and Eve walking in the cool of the night in dialogue with the creator God. In another story at the end of this Gospel of Luke, a thief turns to Jesus and enters into dialogue with the divine with the simple words from the heart, "Jesus, remember me…!" (Oh, how this differs from the rich man's monologue to secure his future!) And his partner in dialogue replies, "Today, you will be with me…we'll be together with my Father…in paradise."

If the real danger in life is living in a monologue with oneself—in the absence of the divine horizon—then the abundance of life lies in entering into dialogue with the divine promises of God in faith and trust. Saint Paul suggests to the spiritual seekers in the tiny church of the Colossians, "So if you have been raised with Christ, seek the things that are above…set your minds on things that are above, not on things that are on earth…for you have died, and your life is hidden with Christ in God."

If we can trust that our lives and our destinies are hidden with Christ in God, then we don't need to babble to ourselves or build bigger barns or live in disregard of other people. We can live the spiritual life, as the rich man could not, in love and care and compassion for the world and all our relationships with the people whom God has given us to cherish. Then, in our pilgrimage on earth, we will know the first signs of paradise.

Chapter 44
The Face of God

*D*oes God have a face? In a parish I once served, a talented artist was teaching an evening Vacation Church School class with a group of adults. Included in the class was the young man who was my associate pastor. The artist handed out paper and magic markers to the class and asked them to draw a picture of God. The next day I was examining the pictures that had been hung in the hallway of the educational area. I came upon the associate pastor's drawing, and I was stunned by what I saw. I was looking at a picture of myself! Actually, I was deeply disturbed—I didn't dare point this out to him—but it did explain why we were having some problems in our working relationship...especially since the picture was not very flattering.

A few days later I noticed his wife looking at the display of pictures, and so I pointed to his drawing of God and asked her, "Who is this?"

She replied, "Oh, that's his father! And you are the spitting image of his father."

At that, I breathed a sigh of relief. But isn't it interesting how our pictures or our perceptions of God are drawn from our life experiences? In fact, they often mask or hide the reality of God. Someone has suggested that the primary and most fundamental task of the church throughout the ages has been the arduous task of transforming our pictures—our perceptions of God. Because we create our pictures of God from within ourselves, we must hear other stories—sometimes shocking stories—from beyond ourselves. We must hear stories from the Word of God.

Have you seen the face of God?

Jacob, a Father of Israel, asserted that he had seen the face of God. Jacob, twin brother of Esau, was the second born, hanging on to the heel of Esau as they moved down the birth canal. Jacob, whose name literally means *supplanter* or *deceiver*, was a wily creature, a wheeler-dealer He was a con man whose whole life had been marked by deception and lies. He had tricked his elderly, nearly blind father, Isaac. Wrapped in animal skins to imitate his hairy brother Esau, and carrying a meal prepared by his mother, he tricked the old man, Isaac, into giving him Esau's birthright. No longer would it read, "The God of Father Abraham, Isaac, and Esau." Because of that trickery, Jacob had to flee from his family and homeland to hide from his brother's wrath. He condemned himself to living a life always on the run.

Jacob's life continued to be, according to the Book of Genesis, one con job after another. He was a bitter, deceitful man struggling to survive in an alien land. Until, as often happens, he grew tired of running from himself. He wanted to meet his brother.

He is camped with his family and all his possessions on the far side of the Jabbok River, not far from where his brother Esau and his troops are encamped. The sun has set, and darkness deepens into night. Jacob sends his family to the other side of the river, closer to Esau's troops.

Was it that he simply wanted to be alone in his tent on this fateful eve? Or was it just another variation on his life of lies, knowing that Esau would not attack the women and children?

Sometime in the depth of that night, lost in a dream world of sleep, sweating, he tosses and turns, throwing off his covers in the frigid night air. He is wrestling with something—with himself? Genesis says Jacob, the deceiver, is wrestling with—not an angel and not a man—but a *being*. And this being transforms the liar and deceiver. The being changes Jacob's name—his very being—in the depth of darkness by the Jabbok. He will henceforth be called *Israel*. A new reality, a new day, a new life has dawned. Make no mistake, the deceiver knew that he was wrestling with his God. He named this place on the Jabbok *Peniel* which means, in Hebrew, "he had seen the face of God." But what did he see?

The next morning, Jacob knows, as the sun burns the hazy fog off the river, that he now aches. (The profoundest transformations of persons are occasioned by woundedness.) Jacob's hip has been damaged in the struggle with the being. For the rest of his new life he would limp…limp all the way into eternity. A different person with a new name, but wounded. He gathers together an offering to appease the wrath of his brother and begins the trek. He crosses the river and limps up the riverbank to encounter his twin brother. Or is it himself?

Squinting into the horizon as he hobbles along, Jacob moves closer toward Esau and his militias and the swords meant for him. Jacob is terrified as he draws closer to the one he has swindled, the brother from whom he had alienated himself so many years earlier, the twin with whom his heart had been synchronized in the womb. The two brothers approach one another, the silence broken only by a breeze rustling in palm trees. Seven times Jacob bows to the earth toward his brother

As Jacob continues to plod forward, slowed by his aching hip, Esau suddenly comes running toward him. Jacob is convinced his brother is about to kill him, but Esau throws his arms around Jacob. Esau buries his head in his brother's neck and kisses him, tears streaming down his face into his beard. And now they are both weeping. The two hearts of the twins are synchronized again.

Jacob introduces his family, as his wives and their children step forward to meet Uncle Esau. This is a moment of incredible joy—this is a reconciling moment of pure grace. Esau turns to his brother and asks, "What is this other company of slaves and animals about?"   "They are a gift, Esau, to find favor with you, my Lord."

Esau sweeps his arm and says (a great line for our times), "I have enough, my brother."

Jacob replies, "Please, take my gift because(and then he finally gets it right, after his self-centered life of deception), truly, to see your face is like seeing the face of God." To see your face is like seeing the face of God!

In the face of Esau, his twin, Jacob sees the magnitude of pure grace and forgiveness. Now he sees for himself, in the midst of his life and face to face with the one he had so deeply sinned against, pure grace and compassion in his brother's hug. Jacob now realizes that what he had seen the night before at Peniel, on the other side of the Jabbok River, was the face of ultimate forgiveness and compassion. That is, the face of God.

Have you seen the face of God? You have, if you have looked into the eyes of Jesus. His are the eyes that weep with joy when we seek reconciliation, realizing how badly we mess up our lives. If you have looked into the eyes of Jesus, through his cross, then you have seen the face of God.

Chapter 45
Wearing Andrew's Sandals

*T*hey were seekers in the fullest sense of that word. Restless and searching. Had they been content with their lives, had they been content with the way their lives were unfolding, they wouldn't have been following that bizarre and strange prophet, John the Baptizer. And perhaps there is a clue here, in the two seekers, which reveals to us what Jesus's ministry is all about.

The Gospel of John tells us that the very first event in Jesus's ministry is an encounter with two seekers. This is an encounter that shakes their lives to the very foundation. In fact, so profound is the encounter, that the two rebuild their lives on a new, thrilling, and frightening foundation of meaning. Such things are known to happen when seekers come face to face with the Lamb of God.

Put yourself in Andrew's sandals and see if they fit. Andrew was a fisherman, sharing the family business with his brother, Simon Peter. They would cast their nets in the darkened Sea of Galilee from sun down to sun up. This was backbreaking labor, but it was a way to survive, a way to eke out a living. And yet, the long and empty nights on the boat could not ease the deeper ache of their hearts. This hidden ache, seldom expressed, seldom confessed to anyone, was an ache for meaning. Andrew and his brother craved a purpose in life to tide them through the long days of mending nets before they launched again out to sea on another, darkened night.

Their own religious faith and practice, wasn't satisfying. Their lives seemed so hollow, so empty and irrelevant and so disconnected from the persistent, nagging ache in their hearts. So Andrew turns to an offbeat religionist, a sectarian prophet from the desert, John the Baptist, whose harsh words seem to break through the glass that encases their lives. Even as he does so, Andrew knows that this prophet isn't the one who is going to ease a heart's ache for meaning.

One day Andrew and another follower of that sectarian prophet find themselves following an even more obscure and unknown rabbi. Jesus catches them questing. He turns and peers into their eyes…all the way into their hearts. And then Jesus stuns them with this foundation-shattering question, "What are you looking for?"

He doesn't ask, "*Who* are you looking for?" Nor does he ask, "*Why* are you following me?" He asks the question that cuts to the heart of human reality, whether several thousand years ago in Palestine or today, *What are you looking for?*

The question, however, is too much—too penetrating and too demanding of self-honesty—so they quickly hide themselves in another question, "Rabbi, by the way, where are you staying?" Idle words that do not conceal the idleness of the heart.

And Jesus replies brilliantly, using no coercion, no dogma, no trite slogan. "Come and see," he says. "Come and enter into your own experience. Test it out. Explore." If the church of Christ today believes that Jesus is who he says he is, this is all the church ever has to do: issue the invitation: Come and see—come and see for yourselves!

But now comes the moment of crisis. The moment of decision. Does the ache for life's meaning outweigh the fear of surrender? Andrew could have answered, "Yeah, I'll stop by tomorrow. Or the next day. Perhaps some other time."

But he didn't.

And, all of a sudden, this man is on life's greatest adventure, because he and his friend go and behold the home of Jesus. Now how long would it take for such an inspection? A few moments perhaps? Six hours, according to John—six hours! A six-hour encounter with the Lamb of God. Six hours of slowly coming to life, of unfreezing from his life's monotony and emptiness. Six hours of sitting beside before the bearer of life's meaning, life's hope, life's excitement.

In the twinkling of an eye, the quickening of a heart, Andrew's empty ache is transformed into a burning passion. A spiritually dead man has been resurrected from the hollow shell of his former life. A butterfly has emerged from the crackling chrysalis. The windows of Andrew's life are thrown open and the winds of a new spirit are wafting through. Overwhelmed with enthusiasm, Andrew and his companion rush to find another with whom to share their conversion—their discovery. Andrew exclaims to Simon, "We have found the Messiah! We have found a life with meaning for you—for me. Do you catch the utter excitement and passion there? Where is it today in this Rabbi's church? Where is the conviction and the passion that accompanies the encounter with the Lamb of God, the encounter that rebuilds lives on new foundations and eases the heart's ache for the life worth living?

I suggest to you that you consider slipping on Andrew's sandals. Heed that gentle yet explosive invitation: Come and see! You might just re-encounter this compelling figure of God anew—this Lamb of God who invited Andrew into the most intimate setting of his own home. We need to spend six hours, not six minutes, with the only person who can transform our ache for meaning into the joy of purpose.

And then test this re-encounter with this daring act: say to another, "I have found the Messiah! I have found life's truth." Can you imagine yourself ever saying that to someone? But you can only do that if you gather up your whole self—open your heart as never before— and let go.

Chapter 46
A Wedding Meditation

You have come to this place at this time, so that the two of you might become one in Christ. But before we rush into invoking God as witness to the promises you will soon make, let's pause briefly to explore a perspective from the scriptures.

I call your attention to the first book of the Hebrew Bible—the Book of Genesis. Genesis means "beginnings," and so what we have before us are very ancient texts that offer well-seasoned insights into the task of marriage. You flinch when I suggested that marriage has a task! The meditation will be brief—the wedding will withstand the day's heat—and the photographer will try to snap a few more candid shots over my protestations. Romance between lovers floods moments such as these, but romantic sentiments must not prevent us from exploring the "task of marriage." Take a deep breath— exhale, and let the anxiety flow away. That way you will hear the rest of the meditation.

There are two versions of the creation story in the second and third chapters of Genesis—we blend them. And so the story goes: God creates the earth, separates light to make night and day. God creates the stars to be lights in the dome of the sky. He proceeds to create the animals and creatures of the earth. And he loves what he creates, boasting about everything as, "Good! I like it!"

And then, for some strange reason—Genesis tells us not why—God says to the heavenly host, "I will make an 'earth creature.'" Maybe God was just feeling lonely and yearning for some human contact. "Adam" means, in original Hebrew, "earth creature." So God creates a single, solitary, sexually undifferentiated *adamah*, a creature of the earth, and he places it in the Garden of Eden. By now God was quite exhausted from all his creativity. But as the afternoon shadows lengthen, God looks down at the Garden and sees that single, solitary earth creature who is just standing there, bewildered.

God says, "This isn't good—I didn't get this right—I need to do something for this lonely creature." God recognizes, for the first time, that something else has crept into his beautiful creation: loneliness. And God says that this loneliness is not good. It will be the greatest challenge to him throughout the ages and eons.

God rises to the challenge of repairing his creation. "I will make a companion for the earth creature." So he creates a woman as the man's companion. In the Hebrew text there is now an *ish* and an *isha*, which means a man and a woman. The woman is a companion, a friend, a fellow journeyer. Is it not interesting that the word "companion" means "to take bread with" in Latin?

The Almighty God's decision is that loneliness is not good for his creatures. It is the earliest rupture in the creation with which God must come to terms and which God must transform. So the task of marriage is to overcome the loneliness of life, a message embedded deep within the earliest scriptures as the fundamental task in life.

A psychiatric patient once said, "The loneliness which is me, reaches out to touch the loneliness which is you." That is the journey you seek to embark upon, hand in hand, from this day forward. You will be most fulfilled in your relationship when you can glimpse those brief moments when you have shared life so deeply, as companions, that the emptiness of loneliness has been taken out of your life's journey and replaced with the love shared between you as wife and husband.

May the creative God of all things go with you as you depart this place!

Chapter 47
The Great Fisherman's Net

Again, he said, the kingdom of heaven is like a net which was thrown into the sea and gathered fish of every kind; when it was full, men drew it ashore and sat down and sorted the good into vessels but threw away the bad. So it will be at the close of the age. The angels will come out and separate the evil from the righteous, and throw them into the furnace of fire where there will be weeping and gnashing of teeth. Have you understood all of this? They said to him, "Oh, yes, Lord!"

Matthew 13: 47-52

*D*id you understand this? I'm not so sure I did. In fact, I have a hunch that the disciples were up to their old tricks again, nodding their heads in agreement, hoping to hide their stupidity. Of course, they hadn't the foggiest notion of what Jesus was saying! One of the most distinguishable characteristics of the gospels is that the disciples, prior to Jesus's death, had not the vaguest idea what was going on. Even when a glimmer of light seemed to dawn on them, it was almost always shallow awareness taken at face value.

So if you kind of frowned when you read this parable of the net, a frown of incomprehension, then you are one solid step ahead of the first hearers of this rather weird parable. I have seldom preached on this strange parable, and whenever I have encountered it, I have simply let it slide on by without even a second glance. And weird it is—the parable has an ominous overtone of terrifying judgment which doesn't fit with all the joy of discovery which precedes it in Matthew's Gospel.

And what a strange way for Jesus to describe the reign of God—the reign of the love which moves the stars and planets on their courses and the love that broke its body on the cross of Golgotha. Rather, he describes the Kingdom of God as some big net thrown into the sea behind a boat, dredging the sea's depths. Jesus implies that this is how it will end. This is what the close of the age and the ultimate fulfillment of our lives will be like: a big old net dragging the vast reaches of the universe. Have you understood all this? Not until I read this parable carefully did I begin to understand—and it is fascinating.

Nowhere in this little parable of the net are fish mentioned in the original Greek text! The Greek word for what the net catches means, simply, *every kind of thing*. The translators were the ones who decided that it was fish. And maybe some fish were caught in the net, some real prize winning beauties, but a lot of other stuff was caught up in that cosmic net, too, as it dipped into the sea of life. Flotsam and jetsam, seaweed and old discarded tires, a few balloon fish and puffers, some of the most uninviting creatures you might imagine— maybe even an eel. The net catches all kinds of things indiscriminately. But what a magnificent image of God Jesus paints, as virtually all of creation is caught up at the close of the age—at the end of time—in the divine net and dragged toward the silvery white beaches of eternity. No judgment is made between what is good or bad, useful or worthless. God's net gathers up every kind and sort of thing. So don't be surprised by who (or what) might be tangled in the net next to you.

And then what happens? When the net was full (and how much does it take to fill God's net with everything that ever was or will be?), it was dragged to the beach. And isn't the beach the best image of eternity? Then the men sit down and gather the good things and dispose of the bad things. And, suddenly, all we moralists and pietists, we do-gooders and believers in ourselves, jump up and clap because we are vindicated in our mistaken belief that we have something good to offer God. Certainly, our scales will glimmer and catch the eye of the Great Fisherman.

But that is wrong! The Greek words here about good things and bad things are not about morality. The words mean *beautiful* and *useful* and *purposeful* in the eye of the beholder. Something gets saved in the good bucket, not because it is morally good, but because it catches the fancy and delight of the Great Fisherman. He does the judging...and *only* at the end of time. So if you are the kind of person who goes around wondering whether you have any intrinsic worth, wondering whether you measure up or your life is worth anything, judging yourself and bad-mouthing yourself, take heart. The Great Fisherman won't even begin judging that until the end of time. Nothing that you have to offer, or fail to offer, will matter. In other words, there are going to be many rusty anchors, discarded tires, broken lobster pots, and clumps of seaweed that delight the Great Fisherman. Therefore, don't judge others, because the Great Fisherman has no intention of doing so until the net is finally dragged through time at eternity.

Simply take heart and remember that God sees the world—all the world including you and me and the rusty anchors and broken lobster pots—through the eyes of Jesus. That is how he looks at each one of us, and he sees beauty and worth which we often cannot even see in ourselves, unless we look through the penetrating lens of Jesus's cross.

But you say, "Aha! Look at how this story ends. Angels pitching the righteous into the bucket and the evil into the furnace of fire." Not very optimistic and encouraging is it? Well, how did the righteous get to be righteous? Simply by the free gift of Jesus's righteousness, offered to every human being simply for the taking. This is the gift of the relentless love of the Great Fisherman. And the unrighteous—how did they turn out so evil and get tossed from the great net into the fire? Even though they received Jesus's righteousness, they decided they just didn't like it. They couldn't stand the thought of not being accepted on their own personal merit or of relying upon the loving glint in the eye of the Great Fisherman.

So where are you going? And where is your life going? Into the bucket or the outer darkness? It will be one or the other, for the net of the Great Fisherman will gather us all in. There is nothing fishy about this deal you're offered—something for nothing. It took everything to make the deal, even the death of the Great Fisherman's Son. You are offered everything. Take it, for *God's* sake! He wants a big catch in his net when he goes on his final fishing trip.

CPSIA information can be obtained
at www.ICGtesting.com
Printed in the USA
LVHW04s2335290918
591838LV00002B/20/P